YORK NOTES

A Midsummer Night's Dream

William Shakespeare

Note by Michael Sherborne

 Longman   York Press

Exterior picture of the Globe Theatre reproduced by permission of the
Raymond Mander and Joe Mitchenson Theatre Collection
Reconstruction of the Globe Theatre interior reprinted from Hodges:
The Globe Restored (1968) by permission of Oxford University Press

Michael Sherborne is hereby identified as author of this work in accordance with
Section 77 of the Copyright, Designs and Patents Act 1988

YORK PRESS
322 Old Brompton Road, London SW5 9JH

PEARSON EDUCATION LIMITED
Edinburgh Gate, Harlow,
Essex CM20 2JE, United Kingdom
Associated companies, branches and representatives throughout the world

First published 2000

ISBN: 978-0-582-42448-7

Designed by Vicki Pacey
Phototypeset by Gem Graphics, Trenance, Mawgan Porth, Cornwall
Colour reproduction and film output by Spectrum Colour

CONTENTS

PART ONE

INTRODUCTION   How to Study a Play   5
                Reading *A Midsummer Night's Dream*   6

PART TWO

SUMMARIES & COMMENTARIES
                Note on the Text   10
                Synopsis   12
                Detailed Summaries   14
                    Act I   14
                    Act II   18
                    Act III   24
                    Act IV   29
                    Act V   33

PART THREE

CRITICAL APPROACHES
                Characterisation   38
                    The Athenian Nobles   39
                    The Craftsmen   44
                    The Fairies   46
                Language & Style   49
                Imagery & Symbolism   51
                Themes   55
                    Love   55
                    Marriage   57
                    Gender   59
                    Theatre   61

PART FOUR

TEXTUAL ANALYSIS
                    Text 1   64
                    Text 2   69
                    Text 3   74

PART FIVE

B ACKGROUND
William Shakespeare's Life   80
Shakespeare's Dramatic Career   81
The Texts of Shakespeare's Plays   82
Shakespeare & The English
Renaissance   84
Shakespeare's Theatre   87
Reading Shakespeare   92
Literary Background   95

PART SIX

C RITICAL HISTORY & BROADER PERSPECTIVES   98
Recent Readings   101

Chronology   104
Literary Terms   106
Author of this Note   110

PART ONE

INTRODUCTION

HOW TO STUDY A PLAY

Studying on your own requires self-discipline and a carefully thought-out work plan in order to be effective.

- Drama is a special kind of writing (the technical term is 'genre') because it needs a performance in the theatre to arrive at a full interpretation of its meaning. Try to imagine that you are a member of the audience when reading the play. Think about how it could be presented on the stage, not just about the words on the page.

- Drama is often about conflict of some sort (which may be below the surface). Identify the conflicts in the play and you will be close to identifying the large ideas or themes which bind all the parts together.

- Make careful notes on themes, character, plot and any subplots of the play.

- Why do you like or dislike the characters in the play? How do your feelings towards them develop and change?

- Playwrights find non-realistic ways of allowing an audience to see into the minds and motives of their characters, for example soliloquy, aside or music. Consider how such dramatic devices are used in the play.

- Think of the playwright writing the play. Why were these particular arrangements of events, characters and speeches chosen?

- Cite exact sources for all quotations, whether from the text itself or from critical commentaries. Wherever possible find your own examples from the play to back up your own opinions.

- Always express your ideas in your own words.

This York Note offers an introduction to *A Midsummer Night's Dream* and cannot substitute for close reading of the text and the study of secondary sources.

A Midsummer Night's Dream has long been a favourite with theatre audiences. Its subject matter of lovers who court each other, defy parental disapproval, break up, make up and finally marry, has a wide appeal because so many people can recognise these experiences, either at first or second hand, but the eventful love story is only one of three **plots**. We are also introduced to a group of amateur actors, preparing a performance for a wedding celebration, whose blundering efforts parody the whole business of putting on a play. Both these actors and the lovers are secretly observed and influenced by a third group, a band of fairies whose supernatural presence adds immeasurably to the spectacle and meaning of *A Midsummer Night's Dream*. The play introduces the three plots one by one, then weaves them into an elaborate theatrical unity.

In doing so, it places considerably greater emphasis on action, and correspondingly less on **characterisation** and verbal **wit**, than practically any other Shakespearean **comedy**, yet *A Midsummer Night's Dream* remains an outstanding artistic achievement. If the characters are not deep, they are strongly drawn and given to behaviour which is engagingly incongruous. Theseus, the legendary slayer of monsters, proves to be a sober, down-to-earth duke with no time for 'antique fables' (V.1.3). His wife-to-be, Hippolyta, queen of the fierce Amazons, is a self-effacing and kindly woman. Although fairies were notorious in folklore for inflicting harm on mortals, here they are represented by a conscientious group of spirits, keen to offer human beings their support. The king and queen of the fairies, Oberon and Titania, may be powerful and otherworldly, but they are also an estranged husband and wife who make wild accusations about each other like the most fallibly human of couples. The Athenian craftsmen have deserted their mundane trades to become actors, determined to put on a show in the face of supernatural intervention, audience derision and, perhaps the greatest impediment of all, their own formidable lack of talent. To cap it all, the constancy of the four young lovers, whose amorous affairs form such a central thread of the story, is turned on and off like a switch by the application of magic eye-drops, with the result that the two men insult and abuse their sweethearts and all four finally descend to extremely unromantic brawling.

As the last point suggests, the play does not lack those darker elements found in all Shakespeare's comedies. Indeed, for a play which many people have assumed was written to commemorate one or more marriages, it has a disconcertingly detached attitude to such matters as the nature of love and the behaviour of lovers. There seems little to choose between Hermia and Helena, Lysander and Demetrius – so much so that generations of students have found themselves mixing them up just as Robin and Oberon do within the play. The attraction the couples feel for each other seems to have nothing to do with the merit of the person being loved, only with the feelings of the person who is in love with them. Love is entirely in the eye of the beholder. In particular, as the two men's views are changed by the application of the fairies' magic juice to their eyes, they fall rapidly in and out of love with the two women, adoring and deriding their partners by turns, while confidently proclaiming all the while that their behaviour is prompted by judgement and reason. Magic even brings about a liaison between the queen of the fairies and a lower-class mortal who has temporarily had his head replaced by that of an ass. When Titania embraces Bottom, Shakespeare seems to be telling us that sexual attraction is not only subjective and irrational, but liable at times to take absurd and perverse forms.

While this unidealistic view of love might be considered shocking, a modern viewer or reader may be even more disturbed by the representation of women in the play. The first scene begins with Hippolyta, the queen of the Amazons, an independent nation of female warriors, about to be married to the man who has defeated her people in a war. Although shortly afterwards we are invited to side with Hermia when she rebels against a forced marriage, and later to sympathise with Titania, the queen of the fairies, when she quarrels with her trickster husband, Oberon, the play consistently assumes that it is ultimately normal and right for the man to be the controlling partner in any male–female relationship.

The play's debunking view of love and gender relations extends to human behaviour and perception in general. In the world of *A Midsummer Night's Dream* human beings are depicted as creatures with limited powers of understanding, which they use to explain away the mysterious forces which really drive and control them. If this is **satire**, however, it is satire of a very genial type. Our self-deceptions are not so much criticised in the play as exposed, accepted and enjoyed.

If *A Midsummer Night's Dream* was simply a love story, the fifth act, which is set after the marriages, would be redundant. One reason for its existence is that the staging of the craftsmen's excruciatingly bad **tragedy**, 'Pyramus and Thisbe', offers a kind of **counterpoint** to the love **theme**. The deaths of Pyramus and Thisbe, strongly reminiscent of those of Romeo and Juliet, show how the lovers' story might have turned out had fate gone against them, reminding us that every **comedy** could easily become a tragedy. The pedestrian devices of language and staging employed in 'Pyramus and Thisbe' also offer a counterpoint to the theatricality of *A Midsummer Night's Dream* itself, for *A Midsummer Night's Dream* is among other things a celebration of the power of the theatre.

When Theseus says that the poet 'gives to airy nothing / A local habitation and a name' (V.1.16–7) he intends it as a criticism, but in this play Shakespeare exults in his creative power to make something out of nothing. He recreates figures of legend like Theseus and the fairies to suit his needs, turns the stage into a magic wood at night by the power of his language, and even convinces the audience that some of the characters are supernatural creatures invisible or smaller than acorns while the human actors are standing before their eyes. This bravura theatricality makes *A Midsummer Night's Dream* a play which has to be seen to be fully appreciated and has led theatre companies to stage it in a wide range of styles and adaptations over the centuries. What will the fairies look like? How will the lovers act out their quarrels? How will Bottom look and behave when he has the head of an ass? Exactly what will go wrong in the staging of 'Pyramus and Thisbe'? There are many potential answers to these questions.

A Midsummer Night's Dream is, above all else, a play about change. The changes from childhood to adulthood, and from singleness to marriage, are central, but the theme also extends to other ways an individual can reach beyond their limited identity, in particular taking part in or watching a play. From this perspective the hero of the drama may well be Bottom, who, for all his deficiencies, has the natural wisdom to accept any role in which he finds himself and the positive spirit to see it through in style. From simple weaver, through magically transformed lover of the fairy queen, to the stage hero Pyramus, Bottom throws himself into the parts he plays with absolute commitment.

Despite its apparent simplicity, then, *A Midsummer Night's Dream* is a drama which has many aspects, open to a variety of interpretations in performance and reading. Do we emphasise one of the three plots, and one set of characters over the others, making it primarily a love story, a knockabout comedy or a fantasy? Do we emphasise laughter, conflict or theatrical spectacle? Which characters do we regard with sympathy and which do we simply find laughable? Is Bottom a fool or a hero? Is Oberon sinister or admirable? Are the four marriages happy unions or should we have reservations about any of them? Is the dominance of men over women challenged or confirmed by what we see? The play allows considerable scope for interpretation. Anyone who stages it has to give a lot of thought to these matters; and so do readers, discovering and experimenting with new meanings each time they open the text, making every engagement with the play a fresh experience.

PART TWO

SUMMARIES & COMMENTARIES

Although *A Midsummer Night's Dream* cannot be dated precisely, we do know it had been written and performed by 1598 because in that year the writer Francis Meres mentioned it in his book *Palladis Tamia*. It is unlikely that it had been written before 1594, the year of Prince Henry's baptism at the Scottish court, when a plan to employ a lion in the celebrations had to be abandoned on grounds of safety, since this incident probably suggested Snout's anxious query, 'Will not the ladies be afeard of the lion?' (III.1.25). The attempts of scholars to find further topical references in the play – for example, Titania's comments on the unseasonal weather in Act II Scene 1 – have proved indecisive. Taking into account stylistic features, such as rhyme, **imagery** and **rhetorical figures**, most people have agreed that the play originated in the period 1594–5, with minor revisions perhaps added later. *Romeo and Juliet* is usually dated at around the same time, and the resemblance between the suicides of those two young lovers and the story of Pyramus and Thisbe suggests that the **comedy** and the **tragedy** are intended to some degree to make up a pair.

A Midsummer Night's Dream was first published in book form in 1600. This version of the text was a so-called 'good' quarto, an edition which was evidently authorised by Shakespeare's theatre company, the Lord Chamberlain's Men. This First Quarto was probably based on the author's own draft manuscript; nonetheless it contained a number of errors. The text was reprinted with minor alterations in 1619 in an edition now referred to as the Second Quarto. In 1623 the play was included in the collected edition of Shakespeare's works known as the First Folio. The Folio version is based on the text of the Second Quarto, but one which had been checked in places against a copy used in the theatre. It therefore corrects some of the earlier mistakes and also offers some indications of how the play was staged. Modern editions of the play are based on the First Quarto, but include some material from the First Folio.

$\mathbf{y}$

Stanley Wells and Gary Taylor's edition of *Shakespeare: The Complete Works* (1986) and Peter Holland's edition of *A Midsummer Night's Dream* for the World's Classics series (1994), both published by Oxford University Press, are unusual in following the First Folio's allocation of speeches in Act V Scene 1. Instead of Philostrate telling Theseus about the entertainments available for the wedding celebrations, Egeus performs this function, while in place of Theseus, Lysander reads out the descriptions from the list. Philostrate does retain one speech in the Folio, but since the point of the revisions seems to be to remove him from the play as a speaking character, this is probably a printer's error.

All the quotations and line references in the present study are taken from the Penguin edition edited by Stanley Wells (1967, revised 1995). Line numbers will sometimes vary in other editions, either because the lines have been counted differently or because the **prose** passages have taken up different amounts of room, depending on the print size and page width. Punctuation, spelling and wording may also vary slightly.

A number of scholars have suggested that *A Midsummer Night's Dream* was written to celebrate an aristocratic wedding, or the combined wedding of two or three couples, and have put forward various celebrations at which it might have first been performed. A minority have even taken the apparent compliment to Queen Elizabeth I (II.1.155–64) to indicate that she was present on the occasion. It is by no means impossible that the play was written for a wedding, with children from the family playing some of the fairies and the happy couple themselves taking the parts later revised as Theseus and Hippolyta. However, there is no evidence for the theory, no-one has found a single example of an Elizabethan wedding celebration at which a play was staged, and those who argue that the use of many boy actors indicates that the play must have been composed for a special occasion have to concede that it was still possible to act it many times on the public stage. The highly unromantic view of love taken by the play is surely a strong point against the wedding theory.

Theseus, Duke of Athens, has conquered Hippolyta, Queen of the Amazons, in battle and is now preparing to marry her. Egeus, an Athenian citizen, comes to him with a complaint that Hermia, his daughter, is refusing to marry Demetrius, the husband he has chosen for her. She instead loves a rival suitor, Lysander. Egeus demands that she do as he orders or be put to death. Theseus offers her a third option, that of becoming a nun. Hermia refuses to change her mind, however, and Lysander casts doubt on Demetrius's suitability as a husband by pointing out that he had previously been in love with another young woman called Helena. While Theseus takes Egeus and Demetrius off to give them some private advice, Lysander persuades Hermia to elope with him. They decide to rendezvous in the wood outside Athens that night. They then reveal their plan to Helena, but she is so besotted with Demetrius that she betrays their secret in order to have an excuse to see him. Demetrius decides to pursue the couple, Helena to follow him.

The four lovers are not alone in the wood. Some Athenian craftsmen, who want to put on a play for the duke's wedding celebrations, have decided to rehearse there that night. The leader of the group is Peter Quince, a carpenter, but their efforts are generally dominated by the exuberant personality of a weaver named Nick Bottom. The craftsmen lack both experience in the art of drama and talent, but are enthusiastically determined to stage their play nonetheless. Oberon and Titania, the king and queen of the fairies, also meet in the wood, each accompanied by their followers. They have fallen out with each other over possession of a human boy, a conflict which has upset the balance of nature, causing severe weather problems for human beings. Titania is caring for the boy and refuses to hand him over to Oberon. The meeting between them leads only to further quarrelling.

Oberon sends his helper, Robin Goodfellow, a puck or goblin, to fetch some magic juice with which to punish Titania. Oberon puts the juice on her eyes while she is asleep, knowing that it will make her fall in love with the next creature she sees. While travelling through the wood, Oberon has observed Demetrius spurning Helena and, thinking to help the young woman, he tells Robin to apply the juice to Demetrius's eyes also. Instead, Robin finds Lysander sleeping, mistakes him for Demetrius and applies the juice to him. When Lysander awakens, he immediately falls in love with the passing Helena and abandons Hermia. Robin, meanwhile, sees the craftsmen rehearsing their play and decides to play a trick on them. He uses magic to give Nick Bottom the head of an ass. After the others have fled in terror at this transformation, Titania awakens and, under the spell of the juice, falls in love with Bottom.

Seeing Demetrius quarrelling with Hermia, who continues to reject him, Oberon realises that Robin's intervention must have misfired. Trying to put the situation right, he applies the juice to Demetrius's eyes when Helena is nearby, but the immediate outcome of this is that Demetrius and Lysander, both of whom have previously been in love with Hermia, are now in love with Helena. She, however, believes that they are mocking and tormenting her, probably with the connivance of Hermia who, joining the others at this point, is baffled to be rejected and insulted by her Lysander. To prevent violence between the lovers, Oberon orders Robin to intervene again, drawing them apart. Once they have grown weary and fallen asleep, Robin puts an antidote juice on Lysander's eyes to take away his love for Helena. Oberon and Robin then remove the magic spells from Titania (who has in the meantime agreed to hand over the boy) and from Bottom. The king and queen of the fairies are reunited.

Theseus and his companions, out early in the morning, discover the four lovers lying asleep in the wood and awaken them. The four explain, in so far as they are able to, their changed feelings. Theseus overrules the objections of Egeus and declares that the two couples shall be married alongside him and Hippolyta. When everyone else has left the wood, Bottom awakens, reflects on his strange 'dream,' then hurries to find the other craftsmen. They are lamenting Bottom's loss and the consequent cancellation of their play when he arrives to announce that all is well.

On the evening of the three marriages, Theseus agrees to the staging of the craftsmen's play, a tragedy called 'Pyramus and Thisbe'. The play is badly written and acted, but in practice its defects make it hugely entertaining and Bottom triumphs in the leading role. When all the humans have gone to bed, the fairies enter the house. They bless those who reside there and their children to come.

ACT I

SCENE 1 Theseus and Hippolyta look ahead to their wedding day. Hermia plans to defy her father and elope with Lysander, but Helena decides to reveal their plan to Lysander's rival, Demetrius

In his palace in Athens, Duke Theseus tells Hippolyta, the Queen of the Amazons, how much he looks forward to their marriage in four days' time. Although he previously made war against her and defeated her in battle, he has now fallen in love with her. The mood is darkened when Egeus arrives, bringing with him his daughter Hermia and her two suitors, Lysander and Demetrius. Hermia is in love with Lysander, but Egeus insists that she either marry Demetrius or be executed. Theseus feels obliged to support the angry father, but suggests a third option, that Hermia might become a nun. Hermia refuses to change her mind, however, and Lysander casts doubt on Demetrius's suitability as a husband by pointing out that he had previously been in love with another young woman called Helena. While Theseus takes Egeus and Demetrius off to give them some private advice, Lysander persuades Hermia to run away with him. They confide their plan to Helena, but she in turn is so in love with Demetrius that she decides to tell him their plans in order to have an excuse to see him.

> The emphasis on marriage and happiness in the opening conversation prepares us for a **comedy**. Theseus's comparison of the moon to a widow spending all her money, frustrating her heir who is eager to inherit it, sets the tone of the play, which exposes the sometimes uncomfortable nature of human motives but does so in a humorous spirit, not a bitter one. That Theseus fought Hippolyta, but now, without explanation, loves her, introduces the **theme** that love is an irrational force, and prefigures the movement of the story from antagonism to harmony. However, the harmony here may not be quite so strong as it at first appears, for it is not clear whether Hippolyta is as happy to be getting married to Theseus as he is to be marrying her. She says little in this scene and what she does say is surprisingly unrevealing of her emotions. In some productions she is played as a loving bride, but in others she is seen to be reluctantly going through the ceremony as part of a peace treaty. Either interpretation is plausible.

There is certainly meant to be some contrast between the attitudes expressed by Theseus and Hippolyta. He is impatient for the wedding night and expresses his frustrations in a joking fashion; she perceives the time to be going quickly and speaks in a quieter, more elevated tone. They even see the moon in opposed ways. He speaks of the moon as waning and compares it to an old woman, she looks ahead to the new moon and compares it to a bow ready to be fired. However, in a play concerned with marriages of opposites, it would be wrong to think that such contrasting states of mind necessarily indicate conflict. They might instead prove to be complementary. The word 'moon' is used three times in the first two speeches and the moon is mentioned seven times in the scene as a whole, establishing it as a key image in this play. (See Imagery & Symbolism.)

Egeus, whose intervention introduces the plot of the young lovers, is a typical figure of comedy, the angry father who obstructs true love. His emphasis on the words 'me,' 'my' and 'mine' (I.1.23–42) quickly establishes his self-centred nature. His accusatory tone, repetitious complaints and unreasonable demands ensure that we have little sympathy or respect for him. Although Theseus feels obliged to support Egeus's rights as a father, he speaks gently to Hermia, gives her four days to reach a final decision and allows her the further option of becoming a nun. In keeping with his own desire for the 'nuptial hour' (I.1.1) and the focus of the play on marriage, he does not make the celibate life sound attractive (the words 'shady … barren … faint … cold … fruitless' and 'thorn', I.1.71–7, are hardly inviting). When Theseus takes Egeus and Demetrius off for some 'private schooling' (I.1.116), we may reasonably assume that he will be critical of their attitude to Hermia, even though he feels obliged to stand up for the men in public. His remark to Hippolyta ('What cheer, my love?' I.1.122) indicates that she is visibly unhappy with the situation. Those who think that she is marrying Theseus with reluctance will suspect that she sees in Hermia's plight a reflection of her own.

The play has begun with two mature lovers looking ahead to their wedding. After the intervening arguments, the focus shifts to a contrasting couple, Hermia and Lysander, who are much younger and whose marriage has been forbidden. While we are meant to feel sympathy for them, their references to examples of thwarted love from history and mythology serve to make them one instance of a general situation and so distance us from strong involvement in their feelings. A similar effect is achieved through formal language such as the balanced **couplets** which, after Helena's arrival, are shared between the two young women ('The more I hate, the more he follows me.' 'The more I love, the more he hateth me' I.1.198–9). The muted conflict which arises between these visibly contrasting women (Hermia is short and dark, Helena tall and blonde) suggests the jealousy and rivalry which will erupt in Act III. When Helena is left alone on the stage, her **soliloquy** referring to Cupid states plainly what will later be shown in action, that love is essentially subjective. Earlier Hermia had wished that her father saw with her eyes (I.1.56). Helena reintroduces this key image of eyes to stress that beauty lies in the eye of the beholder and is therefore liable to be irrational and changeable. Her own irrational decision to tell Demetrius of the elopement reinforces the point and leaves us wondering what will happen as a consequence.

33 **conceits** fancy articles

45 **Immediately** at once, with no right of appeal

89 **Diana** goddess of chastity

171 **Venus' doves** the love goddess's flying chariot was supposedly pulled by doves

173 **Carthage queen** Dido, Queen of Carthage, fell in love with Aeneas (the 'false Trojan') and burned herself to death when he left her

191 **translated** changed

209 **Phoebe** goddess of the moon

SCENE 2   A group of craftsmen from Athens have decided to stage a play, 'Pyramus and Thisbe', to celebrate the marriage of Theseus and Hippolyta. They cast the play and plan the rehearsal

The six craftsmen meet in an unspecified location. Peter Quince, the carpenter, who appears to have written the play, takes charge, giving out the parts and organising the rehearsal. However, his efforts are disrupted by the over-enthusiastic attitude of his leading actor, Nick Bottom, a weaver. Not content with playing the hero, Bottom offers to play all the other parts as well and regrets that there is no role for a raging tyrant which would allow him to perform at full strength. He holds up the proceedings by giving Quince unnecessary advice, demonstrating his acting skills, fussing over what kind of false beard to wear, and sulking briefly when he is not allowed to play all the parts himself. The craftsmen agree to meet for a secret rehearsal that night, a mile outside the town, in the wood.

The second scene forms a strong contrast to the first, both in its content and in its form. Whereas the aristocrats of the first scene speak in verse, the craftsmen speak in prose, with less measured rhythm and more colloquial expressions. When they do attempt to use a more educated vocabulary, they tend to choose the wrong words and inadvertently say something ridiculous. Bottom, for example, confuses 'moderate' with 'aggravate' (I.2.76), which means entirely the opposite, and 'seemly' (or perhaps 'obscurely') with 'obscenely' (I.2.100), which has a different meaning altogether. These mistakes are one source of comedy in the scene. Another is the craftsmen's naïve assumption that their performance will be so convincing that the audience will not be able to tell the difference between a real lion and Snug the joiner in a costume. However, most of the comedy comes from the way that Bottom disrupts the meeting, with Quince largely relegated to the role of 'straight man', patiently explaining his plans when he can get a word in, then flattering Bottom out of his sulk. Bottom's behaviour is rather immature, but he is driven by a real enthusiasm for acting and by enjoyment at putting on a show. If he is overbearing, he is also a natural leader, advising and enthusing the others. The audience is expected to laugh at the craftsmen's ignorance, but there is no mistaking their sincerity, and Bottom's enthusiasm is difficult to resist.

The confusion of genres in the title of 'The most lamentable comedy … of Pyramus and Thisbe' (I.2.11–12) is laughable, but hints also at the nature of *A Midsummer Night's Dream* itself.

Shakespeare's play is a **comedy**, but one which contains serious reflection on the human condition and a potentially **tragic** outcome.

The original sixteenth-century audience would have immediately recognised and enjoyed the craftsmen's parodying of the Elizabethan theatre, with the ranting tyrant's speech and the woman's part played by a man, as well as the actors fussing over their make-up.

Like the first scene, the second ends with plans to go to the wood, leaving the audience wondering whether the lovers and the craftsmen will meet there and how the two **plots** might be linked, but feeling sure that, whatever the details, the outcome is bound to be entertaining.

26 **Ercles** Hercules, the great hero of Greek mythology

31 **Phibbus' car** the chariot of Phoebus Apollo, the sun god

48 **Thisne** this mysterious word is probably Bottom's attempt at a pet name for Thisbe, though some editors have suggested it means 'in this way'

77 **sucking dove** a confusion between 'sitting dove' and 'sucking lamb'

90 **French crowns** French coins, with a double reference to baldness on the crown of the head caused by the so-called 'French disease,' syphilis

93 **con** learn

103 **hold, or cut bowstrings** keep to your promise

ACT II

SCENE 1   The king and queen of the fairies, Oberon and Titania, quarrel in the wood over possession of a human boy. In revenge, Oberon sends his helper Robin for magic juice to put on Titania's eyes, which will make her fall in love with the first creature she sees. When Oberon observes Demetrius spurning Helena, he decides that the juice should be applied to Demetrius's eyes too

The wood is the destination of another group in addition to the craftsmen and the four lovers. A servant of the fairy queen, Titania, is distributing drops of dew there when she encounters Robin Goodfellow, a puck or mischievous goblin, who is the servant of Oberon, the fairy king. Robin warns her that Oberon and his fairies will enter this part of the wood soon and, since the queen and king have quarrelled earlier, there will be a confrontation if Titania and her followers arrive there too. Robin and the fairy talk about the kinds of tricks which a puck commonly plays until they are interrupted by the arrival of Titania and Oberon.

The fairy king and queen do indeed quarrel, she accusing him of a romantic attachment to Hippolyta and he replying that she is equally attached to Theseus. Titania laments that their quarrel has affected the seasons, causing floods and cold which have damaged life for human beings. Oberon says that she can end their quarrel by submitting to him and handing over a young boy he wishes to have for his chief page. She gives a moving account of her friendship with the boy's mother, a worshipper of her cult who died in childbirth, and declares that because of this friendship she will not give up the boy. She then leaves with her followers.

Oberon is determined to punish her for disobedience. He tells Robin of an occasion when he saw an arrow from Cupid's bow fall on a flower and transform it into a magic herb. The juice of this herb will make anyone fall in love with the first creature they see. Oberon sends Robin to fetch the flower, intending to put the liquid on Titania's eyes. While waiting, he sees Demetrius and Helena in the wood. Demetrius has come to prevent the elopement of Hermia and Lysander; Helena's obsessive love for him has caused her to follow him. Seeing Helena scorned by Demetrius, Oberon decides that the juice should be applied to the Athenian's eyes, so that he will be forced to return her love. When Robin brings the flower, Oberon takes some of it to play his trick on Titania and instructs the puck to place some of the remainder on the eyes of Demetrius, whom he will be able to recognise by his Athenian clothes.

> This scene introduces a third group of characters to the play. With the arrival of Helena and Demetrius towards the end of the scene, the separate groups begin to come together, making the audience wonder exactly how the three plots will interweave. The fairies' speeches turn the wood from the everyday location which it has

been so far into a magic nocturnal world where anything might happen.

For all their power, trickery and quarrelling, and the environmental consequences of the last described by Titania, the fairies are much less threatening than they were often reckoned to be in Elizabethan folklore. Their size is generally indicated as being very small – a point established straight away by the fairy's work of placing dew drops in cowslips (II.1.14–15), then reinforced soon after by her mention of elves creeping into acorn cups (II.1.31). Their way of life, which seems to consist largely of caring for natural objects, dancing and playing pranks, is a child-like one, linked explicitly to the tradition of **pastoral** poetry by Titania's references to Corin and Phillida (II.1.66–8).

After the **iambic pentameter** of the aristocrats and the **prose** of the craftsmen, we experience a further contrast in the **verse** of the fairies, which is more varied in **metre** than the speech of the Athenians. The fairies' speeches readily shift into short, rhyming lines and so become song-like, as in the fairy's first speech.

Shakespeare has to establish the world of the fairies very quickly as there was no settled view among people of his time about what such creatures might be like. He does so through the conversation between Robin and the fairy, sketching their respective powers and activities. At the same time, he firmly signals the coming confrontation between Titania and Oberon in order to maintain the momentum of the narrative.

Like the Roman poet Ovid, whose book *Metamorphoses* was a great influence on *A Midsummer Night's Dream* (see Literary Background), Shakespeare uses his supernatural characters to put forward light-hearted mythical explanations of nature. When, for example, cream fails to turn to butter or someone misses their chair and falls, it is because of intervention by the puck (II.1.34–7 and 52–4).

The quarrelling of Titania and Oberon makes them a poor advertisement for the married state to which the other couples in the play look forward so romantically. The disagreements do not actually dispel their exotic glamour, but are sufficiently out of keeping with it to be amusing.

Audiences of Shakespeare's time seem to have had a great fondness for practical jokes – even for ones which to us might seem unduly harsh – so we can assume they would be highly entertained by Robin's mischief-making and the spell which Oberon later casts on Titania. Nonetheless, even they might have had some reservations about the way Titania is treated. Her sympathy for the sufferings of the 'human mortals' (II.1.101) in the unseasonal weather and floods, and her moving account of her love for her dead 'votaress' (II.1.123) which will not allow her to give up the boy to Oberon, must win some audience sympathy.

Titania's long speech beginning 'These are the forgeries of jealousy' (II.1.81–117) is a striking piece of poetry which would be out of place in the mouth of any of the merely human characters in the play. She creates a vivid impression of the countryside through her series of descriptions, and the way she **personifies** the winds, rivers, seasons and moon suggests her supernatural intimacy with the forces of nature. Titania's appearance may be presented in a variety of ways in the theatre through costumes, make-up and lighting effects, but it is really this speech and the succeeding one about the votaress which drive home to the audience that they are not listening to any ordinary character, but to the queen of the fairies.

The same may be said of some of Oberon's speeches (for example, the passage beginning 'I know a bank where the wild thyme blows', II.1.249), although, since none of his contributions are as sustained, none makes quite so great an impression. A modern audience is likely to be puzzled by his remarks about the 'fair vestal' (II.1.148–64). The incident is based upon the kind of pageants staged by noblemen at their country houses when the Queen came to visit them. In 1575, for example, when Elizabeth I stayed with the Earl of Leicester at Kenilworth, she was treated to a parade on water including a boat in the shape of a dolphin and to a spectacular fireworks display. At a royal entertainment of 1581 the Queen watched from a 'Fortress of Perfect Beauty' as courtiers laid siege to her, urging her to surrender to 'virtuous desire'. Elizabeth, however, chose to remain a Virgin Queen, and Oberon's words constitute a compliment to her for this policy. Her chaste nature guards her against the foolish behaviour which love can induce. The point is reinforced shortly afterwards by the behaviour of Helena, whose devotion to Demetrius is so abject that it soon passes beyond sympathy and makes her a laughing stock.

7 **moon's sphere** the moon, planets and stars were thought to be fixed to transparent spheres which rotated about the Earth

10 **pensioners** royal guard

54 **'Tailor'** the expression probably refers to someone falling on their backside or 'tail'

66–8 **Corin and Phillida** names traditionally used for shepherds and shepherdesses in **pastoral**

69 **step** the furthest limit of exploration

78–80 **Perigenia … Aegles … Ariadne … Antiopa** lovers of Theseus during his legendary adventures

92 **continents** banks

98 **nine men's morris** a game with pegs, which could be played outdoors by cutting a pattern of squares in the turf

109 **Hiems** winter **personified** as an old man

123 **votaress** a woman who has taken vows

168 **love in idleness** pansy

192 **wood** maddened

220 **Your virtue is my privilege** your good qualities are my guarantee of safety

231 **Apollo … and Daphne** in the legend, the god Apollo chased the nymph Daphne. She was able to escape his lust only by being turned into a laurel tree

256 **Weed** garment

SCENE 2   **Oberon anoints the eyes of the sleeping Titania. Robin, however, mistakenly applies the juice to Lysander, who suddenly falls in love with Helena and abandons Hermia**

Titania's fairies sing her a lullaby. While she is asleep, Oberon eludes her guards and puts the magic juice on her eyes. Shortly after, Lysander and Hermia, who have become lost, decide to sleep overnight nearby. They are found by Robin who, assuming that Lysander is the Athenian mentioned by Oberon, puts the juice on his eyes. Demetrius and Helena now pass through the same part of the wood, the former running from the latter. Demetrius escapes, but Lysander awakens and falls in love with Helena. She thinks his professions of love are meant to mock her and goes off feeling insulted. He pursues her, abandoning the sleeping Hermia to her fate. At the very end of the scene, Hermia awakens from a nightmare that she is being attacked by a snake and is shocked to find Lysander missing. She fearfully goes in search of him.

The opening of the scene, with Titania issuing orders to the fairies before being sung to sleep, creates a world of pure enchantment, but it is not long before it is disrupted by the arrival of Oberon with the magic juice. His anointing of Titania's eyes and final malicious wish ('Wake when some vile thing is near', II.2.40) make us anxious to see what will happen when she wakes up. Whatever else occurs in the meantime, we never quite forget Titania is sleeping close by. In the original production she would almost certainly have been placed in a curtained recess at the back of the stage (see Shakespeare's Theatre).

The arrival in rapid succession, firstly of Hermia and Lysander, then of Robin, and lastly of Helena and Demetrius, takes us away from the world of enchantment into the world of farce: comedy based on such dramatic features as improbable situations, mistaken identities, sexual infidelities and excruciating coincidences. We are amused by Robin's misinterpretation of Hermia and Lysander's sleeping arrangements (he thinks the distance between them indicates Lysander's negative attitude towards her, but we have seen a few moments earlier that it reflects Hermia's care to preserve her virginity until she is legally married). The greatest source of comedy in the scene, however, is Lysander's instant transformation from Hermia's lover to Helena's, a transformation which none of the characters, least of all Lysander himself, understands. His claim that it is due to the power of 'reason' (II.2.121–2) is hilariously wide of the mark. The joke is capped by Helena's mistaken belief that he is mocking her, which has the paradoxical result that the more passionately he tells her he loves her, the more disgusted with him she becomes. As well as entertaining us in its own right, this situation foreshadows what is likely to occur when Titania awakens, and keeps us looking ahead to that moment. In the event, Shakespeare waits until well into Act III Scene 1, when Titania is finally being pushed out of our thoughts by later developments, before he suddenly brings her back onto the stage, so taking us by surprise.

The awakening of Hermia from her nightmare offers a sudden moment of fear, which gives dramatic contrast to the comedy we have witnessed and reminds us that for the participants this is by no means an amusing situation, but one of great anxiety which could lead to a highly unpleasant outcome.

(See Text 1 of Textual Analysis for a more detailed account of the latter part of this scene.)

4 **reremice** bats
13 **Philomel** the nightingale
36 **ounce** lynx
37 **Pard** leopard
94 **fond** foolish
110 **Transparent** bright, pure, without deceit
138 **gentleness** gentlemanly behaviour

ACT III

SCENE 1   The craftsmen arrive in the wood to rehearse their play, but their performance is disrupted by the mischievous Robin who uses magic to give Bottom the head of an ass. After the others have fled from him in terror, Titania awakens and, under the spell of the magic juice, falls in love with the transformed Bottom

The craftsmen arrive in the wood for their rehearsal, but are once more held up by an interruption from Bottom. This time he is concerned that their play will frighten the female members of the audience because it involves violent deaths. Snout has a similar worry about the presence of a lion on stage. They decide, therefore, to begin the play with a prologue

y

which will explain that they are actors and that the events depicted are not real. Quince has other reservations concerning stagecraft. How will they create a moonlit scene and how will they bring a wall onto the stage? They decide to solve these difficulties by having actors play Moonshine and Wall.

While Bottom and Flute are struggling with their lines, Robin enters invisibly and decides to play a prank on the craftsmen. He gives Bottom the head of an ass, and when Bottom steps out from behind a bush on cue, the other actors flee in terror. Bottom concludes that his friends are trying to make a fool of him, and decides to feign unconcern by walking up and down singing. His tuneless braying awakens Titania who, under the spell of the magic juice, immediately falls in love with him. She introduces herself and orders four fairies to take care of him. Bottom, unfazed by this sequence of events, speaks playfully to the four fairies and goes off with them toward Titania's private part of the wood.

> The craftsmen's assumption that their main problem in putting on a play is that it will be too lifelike is a hilarious misconception. Their literal-minded solutions enhance the joke, and unobtrusively contrast with Shakespeare's own skill in such matters. In particular, their idea of bringing on an actor to personify Moonshine stands in direct opposition to the subtle use of language by which he creates a moonlight atmosphere throughout *A Midsummer Night's Dream*.

> Robin's intervention in the rehearsal guarantees us further fun, and his reference to 'the cradle of the Fairy Queen' (III.1.71) causes us to glance towards the concealed Titania, wondering whether she will be drawn into these events. The disruption of the rehearsal is a great opportunity for comic action. It also raises Bottom in our estimation. If his equanimity reminds us how thick-skinned he is, it equally shows us that he has the knack of accepting whatever happens to him and making the most of it. His observation to Titania that 'reason and love keep little company together nowadays' (III.1.136–7) is considerably more perceptive than the self-deceiving speeches we have recently heard from Lysander. It seems that Bottom has not yet realised he has acquired the head of an ass, as his use of the words 'ass' and 'ass head' (III.1.110 and 114) are amusing precisely because they are unintentionally appropriate.

The exact point at which he does realise what has happened is a matter for judgement and has been placed in performance and critical commentary anywhere between this scene and his awakening in IV.1.

(See Text 2 of Textual Analysis for a more detailed discussion of the opening part of this scene.)

2 **Pat** right on time

90 **Ninnys'** fool's

112 **translated** transformed

124 **cuckoo** because a cuckoo lays its eggs in other birds' nests, a 'cuckold' was a term used for a husband whose wife had a sexual relationship with another man. Someone who feared he might be a cuckold would naturally find the cuckoo's song a displeasing sound

139 **gleek upon occasion** make a satirical joke when the opportunity arises

195 **enforcèd** the meaning is ambiguous. It is usually interpreted as violated or raped, but could actually have the opposite sense of compelled or unwanted

SCENE 2   **Demetrius has met with Hermia, who continues to reject his love. Oberon observes them quarrelling and realises that Robin's intervention has misfired. Trying to put the situation right, he applies the juice to Demetrius's eyes when Helena is nearby, but the immediate outcome of this is that Demetrius and Lysander become rivals for Helena's love, while she believes that both of them are tormenting her, probably with the connivance of Hermia, who joins them during the quarrel. To prevent violence, Oberon orders Robin to intervene again, drawing the lovers apart. Once they have grown weary and fallen asleep, Robin puts an antidote juice on Lysander's eyes to take away his love for Helena**

As Titania and Bottom leave the stage, Oberon comes on wondering with what creature Titania has fallen in love. Robin enters and enlightens him, telling him about the trick he has played on the craftsmen and stating that he has solved the problem of the Athenian lovers. This last boast is immediately punctured when Hermia and Demetrius enter, quarrelling furiously – she concerned about what has happened to

Lysander, he determined to pursue his own love for her. When she storms off, having half-convinced herself that Demetrius has killed Lysander, and he has given up pursuing her and lain down to sleep, Oberon chastises Robin for his mistake and orders him to lure Helena to where they are. In the meantime, Oberon anoints the eyes of Demetrius with the juice.

Helena arrives pursued by Lysander and, to the mischievous Robin's delight, when Demetrius awakens both men become rivals for Helena's love. She refuses to believe that their expressions of affection are anything other than mockery of her. This comedy of cross-purposes is raised to even greater heights of absurdity when Hermia re-enters. She cannot understand why Lysander claims that he no longer loves her, nor why Helena believes her to be a collaborator in her torment. However, as Lysander and Demetrius repeatedly insult her, she begins to think that she is the victim of a plot and that it is Helena who has been responsible for turning the two men against her.

While Lysander and Demetrius go off to fight a duel, Helena runs away in fear of Hermia's anger, leaving Hermia utterly confused by the rapid turn of events. Like the audience, Robin finds the lovers' behaviour hugely entertaining, but Oberon is not at all pleased with the way his plans have turned out. He orders Robin to take further measures, this time drawing the two men apart by darkening their vision and imitating their voices. Once the puck has separated them, he will be able to use an antidote juice to restore Lysander's love for Hermia. Oberon will in the meantime make a new effort to obtain the boy from Titania and, when this has been achieved, will release her from the spell. Robin is concerned that these plans should be carried out before the dawn. Oberon reassures him that as good spirits they do not have to fear the sunrise, but he agrees that it would be best to put things right before the new day begins. Robin carries out his mission, reassuring himself and the audience that all will now be well.

> Throughout this scene the audience derive a lot of enjoyment from knowing more than the characters do. Not one of the characters fully understands what is going on and we are entertained by their astonishment when they suddenly learn that all is not as they had thought. When Robin enters, we share his jollity as he summarises

for Oberon the results of his pranks, incidentally allowing Shakespeare to recreate Robin's disruption of the rehearsal in such a way as to draw the best possible picture of it for the audience, but we know that Robin's confidence that he has solved the problem of the Athenian lovers will soon prove to be misplaced. Even as he is speaking, Hermia and Demetrius are coming on stage and Robin turns from being the instigator of misunderstanding to yet another victim of it.

The confrontation between Hermia and Demetrius, which out of its context might seem painful and ominous, becomes amusing for us because we know that the whole dispute is misconceived and temporary, a point reinforced by the presence of Oberon and Robin whom we can count upon to put it right. Oberon's subsequent anger and Robin's rather anxious compliance with his orders ('I go, I go – look how I go –' III.2.100) constitute a second comic double-act, which gives us a respite from the lovers' confusion. However, the arrival of Helena and Lysander, followed by the return of Hermia, escalates the degree of misunderstandings between the four lovers to a comic crescendo, which achieves the maximum permutation of confusion between them.

Not observing his rival asleep nearby, Lysander reminds Helena that Demetrius loves Hermia. At this very moment Demetrius starts up and extravagantly declares his love for Helena instead. The more Lysander and Demetrius insist upon their love for Helena, the more rejected by them she feels and the more angry and contemptuous she becomes. The more Hermia is insulted by Lysander and Demetrius, the more Helena believes her to be in league with them. Hermia, meanwhile, is soon convinced of the opposite, that the others are in league against her, and a total breakdown of relationships is reached.

Comedy is preserved by the benevolent presence of Oberon, who explains to Robin how things may be put right with such confidence that we have no fear of a **tragic** ending. The healthy country **imagery** with which he characterises himself and the other good spirits, rejecting the dark, ghostly imagery offered by Robin, which probably reflects what the original audience would have associated with fairies, adds to the sense that we are moving toward a positive conclusion. We are both relieved and entertained as we see Robin tricking the four into behaving as he wishes before commenting on the happy outcome in rustic terms that follow on from the natural images used by Oberon.

(See Text 3 of Textual Analysis for further discussion of this scene.)

17 **nole** head

28 **senseless** inanimate

30 **From yielders all things catch** everything is torn from those who have lost control

188 **oes and eyes** stars

203 **artificial** skilful

213 **like coats in heraldry** the two girls were united as the coats of arms of a man and a woman were combined under one crest when they married

220/344 **amazed** confused, as though lost in a maze

317 **simple and ... fond** foolish

355 **Hie** go

356 **welkin** sky

357 **Acheron** a river in Hades (Hell)

380 **Aurora's harbinger** the dawn's herald, the morning star

ACT IV

SCENE 1   **Oberon and Robin remove the magic spells from Titania and Bottom, and the king and queen of the fairies are reunited. Theseus and his companions, out early in the morning, discover the four lovers, who explain their changed feelings. Theseus overrules the objections of Egeus and declares that the two young couples shall be married alongside him and Hippolyta. When everyone else has left, Bottom awakens and reflects on his strange 'dream'**

The scene opens with a picture of absurdity: Titania doting on the ass-headed Bottom, while fairies rush to do his bidding. When Bottom and Titania have fallen asleep in an embrace, Oberon and Robin enter.

Oberon now feels sorry for Titania, especially since she has conceded that he can have the boy he wished for as his page, and he uses the antidote ('Dian's bud') to release her from the spell of 'Cupid's flower'. Restored to her normal self, she is horrified at her recent love for Bottom. Robin removes Bottom's ass's head, and the king and queen of the fairies dance in celebration of their reunion, Oberon promising that they will dance again tomorrow, blessing Theseus's house after his marriage.

The fairies are not long gone when Theseus himself arrives on the scene, accompanied by Hippolyta, Egeus and others. Theseus is taking pleasure in showing off to Hippolyta his hunting dogs, which, although they are slow at hunting, have been bred to bark in impressive harmony with one another. In doing so, he discovers the four lovers sleeping in the wood and has his hunting horns blown to awaken them. He asks how it is that the two rivals, Lysander and Demetrius, have become so friendly. They are unable to give a clear account of the events of the previous night, but Lysander confesses that he and Hermia were attempting to elope. Egeus interrupts to call for Lysander to be punished, appealing to Demetrius for support. However, Demetrius explains that he no longer loves Hermia, but once again loves Helena. Theseus is delighted with this outcome. He overrules Egeus and declares that the two couples shall be married with him and Hippolyta. After the aristocratic party has left, with the four lovers following in the rear still feeling dazed and confused, Bottom, who has been overlooked by them all, awakens.

At first he thinks he has fallen asleep during the rehearsal and calls out for his companions; then he remembers his transformation into an ass loved by the queen of the fairies, although these events are so improbable and in some respects embarrassing that he can hardly speak them aloud, even to himself. He decides to have a song written by Peter Quince, telling the story of his adventures, and considers singing it as part of their play, perhaps as a dramatic accompaniment to Thisbe's death.

> The dalliance of Titania and Bottom parodies what must have been every Elizabethan man's daydream, to be loved by a queen and waited upon by her servants. Bottom affects the courtly French term 'Monsieur' (IV.1.8), but cannot conceal his hairy face, big ears and primitive taste in music ('the tongs and the bones', IV.1.29).

Even as we are amused by Bottom's incongruous situation, we are nonetheless likely to be moved by Titania's adoration of him and to be reminded yet again that love is in the eye of the beholder.

When Oberon and Robin enter and restore the normal order of things, we are pleased to see the king and queen of the fairies reunited, especially since we know that their relationship is **symbolic** of harmony in nature, yet it is difficult not to resent Oberon's treatment of Titania. Throughout the play he seems totally confident of his right to interfere in the lives of others. Here he tricks and humiliates his wife when she will not give him what he wants, then casually orders her to be silent ('Silence awhile!' IV.1.79). This is an extreme image of masculine control. In keeping with the play's fondness for pairings, however, the presence of the dominating Oberon is balanced by that of the grotesque victim Bottom, a man who is partly animal and who has achieved happiness and respect only because a woman's love has lifted him above himself. Oberon is the more impressive figure, but he is not after all a human being as Bottom is.

The dance of Oberon and Titania **symbolises** the restoration of the order of nature, pictured for centuries as a cosmic dance of the elements – for example, in John Davies's contemporary poem *Orchestra*, published in 1596. After this musical interlude, Robin, then later Theseus, use the **imagery** of morning and daylight to lead us out of the dream-like night back into the normal world where the court party finds the four young lovers sleeping. The baying of the dogs, each noisy, but together forming a harmony ('so musical a discord, such sweet thunder', IV.1.117), seems to parallel the way that **comedy** takes disturbing, disruptive events and resolves them into a pleasing unity, and so signals to the audience that we are moving toward the conclusion of the play. Certainly the ranting of Egeus, reluctantly respected by Theseus in Act I Scene 1, is dismissed out of hand here. The 'law of Athens ... Which by no means we may extenuate' (I.1.119–20) suddenly becomes much more malleable, and with the simple line, 'Egeus, I will overbear your will' (IV.1.178), Theseus reverses his earlier decision and permits a happy ending. Characteristically,

Shakespeare is unconcerned with probability or realism at this turning point of the story.

It is left to Bottom to comment on what has taken place during the night. Groping for words to express his experiences, he offers a garbled variation on a passage from St Paul's First Epistle to the Corinthians, another example of how the play brings together opposites, in this case the solemn words of scripture, scrambled and applied to the experiences of a comical character. In the Bishops' Bible, the translation known to Shakespeare, the relevant words are, 'The eye hath not seen, and the ear hath not heard, neither have entered into the heart of man, the things which God hath prepared for them that love him' (1 Corinthians 2:9). Although we are not expected to take the antics of the fairies too seriously, they are one way of conceiving the cosmic forces which drive existence and empower love, and in his way Bottom has glimpsed something of this, even though his ability to express it is limited to an ill-conceived 'ballad', which he proposes to insert into 'Pyramus and Thisbe' in the place where it will do the most damage to the drama.

19 **neaf** fist
31 **peck** a measure equivalent to two gallons
138 **Saint Valentine** birds were supposed to choose their mates on St Valentine's Day, 14 February
188 **parted** out of focus with each other

SCENE 2   **The other craftsmen are lamenting Bottom's loss and the consequent cancellation of their play, when he arrives to announce that all is well and their play may be staged after all**

We are able to enjoy the disappointment of the craftsmen because, once again knowing more than they do, we confidently expect Bottom to appear suddenly and change the atmosphere. We are not disappointed. Bottom is characteristically torn between boasting of his adventures and keeping them a tantalising mystery which will hold the others' attention upon him – or is it perhaps that he wants to tell them his experiences, but does not know how to put them into words? In any case, he has more urgent news, that 'Pyramus and Thisbe' is 'preferred' (IV.2.34). This seems to mean only that the play has been accepted by Philostrate, the Master of the Revels, as a possible entertainment, since Theseus does not finally decide upon it until the next scene. Bottom, however, is full of confidence and the audience can have little doubt that the play will now be staged.

4 **transported** abducted by supernatural forces
32 **pumps** light, low-soled shoes

ACT V

SCENE 1   On the evening of the three marriages, Theseus agrees to the staging of 'Pyramus and Thisbe'. The play is badly written and acted, but in practice its defects only add to its entertainment value. When all the humans have gone to bed, the fairies enter the house and bless those who reside there and their children to come. Robin remains behind to deliver an epilogue

The play concludes in the place where it commenced, the palace in Athens. Theseus has now heard the lovers' accounts of their adventures in the forest, which apparently contain some suggestion of supernatural intervention, and expresses his scepticism to Hippolyta, classifying lovers with poets and madmen as people deluded by their own imaginations. She is more impressed by their testimony, however, noting its consistency and conviction.

When the lovers have joined them, Theseus asks Philostrate what kinds of entertainment are available to pass the time until they retire. Despite Philostrate's warning that the craftsmen have no talent for the theatre, Theseus decides the three couples will see 'Pyramus and Thisbe,' arguing that the actors' good intentions will outweigh their weaknesses. He reassures Hippolyta that the performance will not be an embarrassment because as Duke of Athens he is used to setting people at ease and showing them his appreciation, even when they are so overwhelmed by taking part in an important occasion that they become incoherent. Despite this statement, he, Lysander and Demetrius, and to a lesser extent Hippolyta herself, keep up a sarcastic commentary throughout the craftsmen's performance. Of the actors, only Bottom has the self-confidence to answer them back and, out of the ill-written and badly plotted play, he emerges as an absurd but spirited comic hero. The play ends in a dance, after which the couples retire to bed.

The fairies now enter the house, Robin first, then Oberon and Titania with their followers. They bless the house, those who are spending their wedding night there, and the children they will have. The fairies sing and dance. When the others have dispersed around the house, Robin remains to deliver the epilogue to the actual audience in the theatre. He tells them that, if the play has not been to their liking, they should dismiss it as a mere dream, but if they applaud, they will be rewarded in the future with a better play.

> Theseus's description of lovers, poets and madmen as equally deluded is amusing, but clearly unfair, since creative writers are able to make a distinction between their own imaginings and the external world, and most lovers are 'frantic' (V.1.10) only in valuing the person they love more highly than others do, not in experiencing hallucinations about them. Since Theseus himself is a lover, his remarks to Hippolyta about the delusive nature of love are somewhat tactless, even if intended to be ironic. His remarks about poetry are equally unlikely to impress an audience who have enjoyed and appreciated the fairy world created by Shakespeare. The fairies are not the products of a defective brain, but of skilfully crafted art. Neither their author nor the audience believe them to be literally real, but they may believe them to have a 'strange and admirable' significance (V.1.27) within the context of the play. The audience know, in addition, that Theseus himself is not Theseus but an actor who is merely pretending to be a character from 'antique fables' (V.1.3) – and they know it without any need for the clumsy disclaimers which the craftsmen think are necessary to prevent confusions between art and life.

> Philostrate offers Theseus four pieces of entertainment. The first three, with their themes of violence, poverty and death, are clearly unsuitable for a wedding celebration. The initial offering

is perhaps the worst of all. Not only is it to be presented by the inappropriate figure of a eunuch, but as an educated Elizabethan would probably have known, Theseus himself took part in the gruesome battle with the Centaurs and, in so doing, disrupted a wedding feast. After these ill-judged proposals, the paradoxical claims made for 'Pyramus and Thisbe,' apparently caused by Quince's uncertain vocabulary ('*tedious brief ... tragical mirth*', V.1.56–7), seem refreshingly intriguing. Philostrate wittily resolves these paradoxes in his account of the play and cautions Theseus against seeing it, but his admission that the rehearsal made him cry with laughter convinces Theseus that it will be amusing, which is all he desires of it. Hippolyta's concern that the actors may be humiliated shows us her caring nature, and Theseus too, although his account of how he deals with tongue-tied dignitaries might be considered rather boastful, is lifted in our estimation by his care for others and his perception that glib speeches and sincerity do not always go together.

After his thoughtful remarks, it is disconcerting to see that he, Hippolyta, Lysander and Demetrius do in fact make sarcastic or negative comments throughout the performance, many if not all of them audible to the actors. Moonshine, in particular, has his contribution ruined by carping interruptions. (Hippolyta's 'I am aweary of this moon. Would he would change', V.1.244–5, oddly echoes Theseus's sentiments in the opening lines of the play, bringing us full circle.) It may be that Elizabethan audiences did commonly behave in this way, and that we should take this example as a comparatively restrained and supportive one. In any case, it gives Bottom the chance to show his mettle. Instead of trying to ignore the comments, he boldly steps out of role and explains to the audience, in as patronising a manner as their own, what it is they are supposed to be appreciating. Back in role, he throws himself into the part of Pyramus with such enthusiasm that Hippolyta cannot help feeling sorry for the character. Unlike the others, Hermia and Helena do not join in the mockery of the play. Would it be impolite for them as mere women to join in with the men and the Duchess, or is it, as some critics think, that they are still subdued by the experiences which they have recently gone through, being rejected and insulted by the men they love?

'Pyramus and Thisbe' is a masterpiece of incompetence. Quince delivers the Prologue so badly that he manages to consistently reverse its meaning. Elsewhere we encounter mispronunciation ('Ninny's tomb', V.1.199), padded lines ('At the which let no man wonder', V.1.133), extravagant repetitions ('die, die, die, die, die', V.1.298), inept **personifications** ('Thanks, courteous wall' V.1.175), crude **alliteration** ('Quail, crush, conclude, and quell', V.1.279), ill-chosen **similes** and **metaphors** ('His eyes were green as leeks', V.1.327), incongruities of tone ('O dear!', V.1.273) and garbled references to mythology. The short lines adopted at the **tragic** climax of the play speed up the rhythm and emphasise the rhymes in a way suitable only for **comedy**. There are numerous splendid opportunities for bad acting which different productions will develop in their own ways, but it is worth noting one which was recorded in the 1600s, in a remark in Edward Sharpham's play *The Fleire*, since it may well preserve stage business from Shakespeare's original production. When she comes to kill herself, Thisbe cannot find Pyramus's sword and has to make do instead with stabbing herself to death with his scabbard. Amidst all this comedy, 'Pyramus and Thisbe' does have an underlying seriousness, however. Its story, paralleling that of *Romeo and Juliet*, shows how young love which defies parental authority can lead to destruction. Lysander and Demetrius, as they laugh at the play, fail to recall how close they came to killing each other on a similar moonlit night only twenty-four hours before. The play concludes with singing and dancing, which here, as throughout *A Midsummer Night's Dream*, creates a sense of celebration and natural harmony.

Theseus's remark that it is almost 'fairy time' (V.1.354) is probably a joke at the young lovers' expense. However, no sooner has he left the stage than the fairies do enter, reunited, to bless the three marriages. Robin again introduces dark, ghostly **imagery**, but typically of the play, this is soon set aside in favour of the reassuring, domestic imagery of fireplaces and beds. The four lovers whom Egeus originally marched onto the stage as children have left the stage as adults and are now themselves about to become parents. Oberon concludes the main part of the play by blessing them and their children to come.

When Oberon has finished, Robin's remarks switch the focus of our attention from the events on stage to the relationship between play and audience, inviting us to decide how we shall come to terms with *A Midsummer Night's Dream* and how we shall assess it. Is our experience of it as idle as a dream or something more serious? Does it deserve hissing ('the serpent's tongue', V.1.423) or applause ('your hands', V.1.427)?

11 **a brow of Egypt** the dark-skinned face of a gypsy

32 **masques** spectacular courtly entertainments featuring drama and dance

48 ***Bacchanals*** women of Thrace who followed the cult of Bacchus, the god of wine, and in a drunken ecstasy tore to pieces the poet-musician Orpheus

52 ***thrice three Muses*** the nine goddesses of the arts

80 **conned** learned

90 **take what they mistake** accept positively, and correct in our minds, what they get wrong

96 **periods** full stops

161 **sinister** left

179–80 **curse again** return the curse

193–5 **Limander ... Helen ... Shafalus ... Procrus** mistakes for Leander, Hero, Cephalus and Procris

234 **horns on his head** a 'cuckold,' who was deceived by his wife, was supposed to acquire horns on his head

276 **Furies** supernatural creatures who pursued the guilty in search of vengeance

277 **Fates** three goddesses in Greek mythology who in turn span the thread of life, drew it out and finally cut it

278 **Cut thread and thrum** cut the weaver's thread and its tufted end, i.e. both the good and the valueless, the whole of his life

328 **sisters three** the Fates

344 **Bergomask dance** a country dance

374 **triple Hecate** the goddess called Diana on Earth was known in the heavens as Luna, Phoebe or Cynthia, and in Hell as Proserpina or Hecate

423 **serpent's tongue** the hostile hissing of the audience, as opposed to their clapping 'hands' in applause

PART THREE

CRITICAL APPROACHES

CHARACTERISATION

The characters in *A Midsummer Night's Dream* occur in three groups. The first to appear on stage are the Athenian nobles, who soon sub-divide themselves into the four lovers and the rest of the court. Next, the Athenian craftsmen make an appearance; finally, the fairies. Although there is considerable interaction between them as the story unfolds, the three groups remain throughout remarkably distinct.

One major area of difference between them lies in their respective status and power, which is reflected in their unequal knowledge of each other. The craftsmen, at the bottom of the hierarchy, have no insight into or power over the higher groups, whereas the nobles and the fairies can readily watch, comment upon and influence them. Elevated above the nobles by their supernatural powers, the fairies are also able to monitor them and intervene in their affairs, while the nobles in return are barely aware of the fairies' existence. In the position of greatest superiority, Oberon and his assistant Robin are the most powerful members of the fairy group, observing and controlling everyone – including the fairy queen, Titania – and making themselves invisible to all but the theatre audience whenever they wish.

Each of the three groups is made up, for the most part, of characters who are fixed in role. Only Nick Bottom and the puck Robin Goodfellow have a playful desire to experience others' identities which allows them to cross temporarily from their own group to another one. Robin can imitate anything animal, vegetable or human, including the voices of Lysander and Demetrius, while Bottom finds himself drawn into the world of the fairies by Robin's spells where he even usurps Oberon's place as Titania's lover.

On stage it is possible to create further overlap between the groups by following Bottom's wish in Act I Scene 2 and having actors take more than one part. It is impossible to know how such matters would have been dealt with in Shakespeare's original productions, but in some modern performances Theseus and Oberon have been played by the same actor and Hippolyta and Titania by the same actress. Peter Brooks's 1970 version went one step further and also cast the same actor as Philostrate and the puck. When such pairings are made, they inevitably affect our interpretation of the play. The doublings cited above, for example, suggest that the fairy world is in some sense a projection of the Athenians' group subconscious, with the fairies as dream-selves of the mortals, manifesting and working out their ambivalent feelings towards each other in fantasy form through the night.

THE ATHENIAN NOBLES

THESEUS

Theseus, Hippolyta and Egeus seem quite straightforward characters in themselves, but each demands some additional piece of interpretation which slightly complicates our view of them. In the case of Theseus, this arises because of his existence as a figure in mythology. Before we see him on stage we already know him by reputation as a great hero, famous for such deeds as the slaying of the Minotaur. In defiance of our expectations, his actions within the play are not those of a heroic warrior, but of a respectable, middle-aged gentleman. Despite a number of references to his legendary past, Theseus cuts a distinctly unromantic figure, sober in action, moderate (even complacent) in tone, and positively scornful of lovers' passions and 'antique fables' (V.1.3). He is always benign and sensible, restraining the excesses of Egeus, giving eventual support to the lovers, presiding over the marriage festivities and bestowing recognition on the craftsmen for their dramatic efforts. He sensibly avoids confrontations and seeks harmony, even to the extent of breeding his dogs to bark in a harmonious manner. In all this he is far from the ruthless killer and faithless lover of legend.

How far, then, should we allow our knowledge of Theseus outside the play to affect our response to him within it? Oberon's reference to his promiscuous past (II.1.77–80) ensures that we cannot ignore the point. Shakespeare probably intends Theseus's divergence from his heroic legend to be an incidental comic feature of the play, but some recent critics have suggested that the duke is a man under whose respectable surface lurk exotic knowledge and passions which have been repressed only temporarily.

HIPPOLYTA

Hippolyta, too, is a more elusive character than she may at first appear. Her visible concern for Hermia in Act I Scene 1, her open-mindedness toward the story of the lovers' adventures in the wood, and her fear lest the craftsmen be humiliated in their performance, mark her out as a woman who is thoughtful and kind, and also ready to defer to her husband's judgement when he responds to these concerns. However, in a play which contains such self-assertive women as Hermia, Titania and even (through Oberon's tribute to her as an 'imperial votaress', II.1.163) Elizabeth I, such passive behaviour seems surprising. Hippolyta is, after all, the Queen of the Amazons, leader of a nation of female warriors, and Titania characterises her with the vigorous word 'bouncing' (II.1.70).

The answer may lie in the Elizabethans' traditional view of the Amazons as a **symbol** of passions needing to be governed by reason, just as women (so it was assumed) needed to be governed by men. This view of the Amazons is found, for example, in Edmund Spenser's poem *The Faerie Queene* (1596) and in *The Two Noble Kinsmen* (1613), a play of which Shakespeare is thought to be joint-author. The defeat of the Amazons by Theseus and the marriage of their queen, Hippolyta, to her conqueror may be intended as a reassurance that this play will not ultimately support emotional and/or female rebellion against society. Indeed, as the action progresses, we see Oberon defeat Titania, and Hermia succeeds in defying her unjust father only through the intervention of two superior male authority figures, Oberon and Theseus, after which she apparently reverts to wifely obedience.

If Hippolyta symbolises female deference and possibly also the subordination of emotion to reason, there still remains the basic problem of how she is to be played as an individual character. Her long silences and her slight disagreements with Theseus when she does speak may indicate some animosity between the two of them. In Act I Scene 1 she implies that she is in no hurry for their wedding night. In Act IV Scene 1 she responds coolly to Theseus's praise of his hunting dogs by praising someone else's. In Act V Scene 1 she questions Theseus's interpretation of the lovers' stories and is generally unappreciative of the play he has chosen for their entertainment. While it is possible for an actress to play Hippolyta as a doting fiancee and wife, the text accommodates a tenser relationship and in some productions she has successfully been presented

Y

as an unwilling captive, resentful of a military defeat and a diplomatic marriage. In a version staged in San Francisco in 1966, she even made her first entry as a caged prisoner – although this emphasis on her disaffection is surely too extreme.

EGEUS

Egeus is a stock character of comedy, the self-righteous father determined to thwart his daughter's choice of husband. In most editions and performances he appears in the play only twice, once in the opening scene to threaten Hermia with execution if she does not marry Demetrius, then again in Act IV Scene 1 to accept Theseus's ruling that she can marry Lysander after all. The contrast between the sustained complaining of his first appearance and the rapid capitulation of the second may seem surprising, but happens because he is a merely functional character, included in the play not for his intrinsic interest but to advance the story. If the actor who plays him avoids drawing attention to himself when he is not speaking, there should be no sense of contradiction in his behaviour. Alternatively, recalling that Theseus has given Egeus 'some private schooling' (I.1.116) between his two appearances – presumably criticising his unreasonable treatment of Hermia – we can imagine a performance where Theseus's line, 'Egeus, I will overbear your will' (IV.1.178) is delivered in such a forceful manner that no Athenian citizen would dare to contradict it. The actor playing Egeus could then behave in a comically deflated or touchingly sad manner, according to preference.

Versions of the play where Egeus reappears in Act V (see Note on the Text at the start of 'Summaries & Commentaries') demand a similar treatment. By speaking politely to Theseus and Lysander, Egeus can demonstrate that he has been reconciled to Hermia's choice of husband, or by speaking his lines with wounded dignity he can suggest the opposite. As Barbara Hodgdon has pointed out in her article 'Gaining a Father: The Role of Egeus in the Quarto and the Folio' (see Dutton 1996, in Critical History & Broader Perspectives, Recent Readings), if Egeus is included in Act V his feelings will inevitably be revealed by his actions when he leaves the stage. Does he fall in behind Theseus and Hippolyta, or does he accompany Hermia and Lysander, perhaps offering them a hug and a handshake as the three depart?

HERMIA, HELENA, LYSANDER, DEMETRIUS

The four lovers have somewhat limited developments as characters. This helps to make their changes of allegiance dramatically effective, since there is so little to choose between them. More personality would only have complicated our reactions. The lovers use the standard language of Elizabethan love poetry, featuring exaggerated comparisons of the beloved to objects in nature, mythology and religion, except when they quarrel and drop, amusingly, into a lower **register** of abusiveness. Contrast Demetrius's speech to Helena beginning 'O Helen, goddess, nymph, perfect, divine' (III.2.137) with his earlier, 'I am sick when I do look on thee' (II.1.212).

Hermia is the darker and shorter of the two young women. 'Who will not change a raven for a dove?' asks Lysander (II.2.120), contrasting her complexion and hair colour with Helena's. Later he calls Hermia an 'Ethiope' and a 'tawny Tartar' (III.2.257 and 264), a 'dwarf', a 'bead' and an 'acorn' (III.2.328–30). Dark hair and skin were considered unfashionable in this period, but before the magic juice distorts their reactions both men perceive Hermia as highly attractive. It may be her unfashionable appearance that has encouraged Hermia to be self-assertive, or perhaps she just takes after her father Egeus, who does not seem bashful in expressing his opinions. In the first scene she is prepared to defy not only her father but Duke Theseus. Although she inserts the maidenly disclaimer, 'I know not by what power I am made bold' (I.1.59), she has plenty of reserves of courage left shortly afterwards to agree to elope with Lysander. On her arrival in the forest, she firmly insists that Lysander sleeps separately from her. When she thinks Demetrius may have killed Lysander she becomes highly aggressive ('Out, dog! Out, cur!', III.2.65) and when she thinks that Helena has stolen Lysander's love she threatens her with violence ('my nails can reach unto thine eyes', III.2.298). She is rather mercurial in temperament, and her name appropriately enough seems to derive from that of Hermes, the ever-moving messenger of the Greek gods, known to the Romans as Mercury.

Helena's name means Light, fittingly as she is fair in colouring, as well as tall. She seems at first to be confident of her own attractiveness ('Through Athens I am thought as fair as she', I.1.227), but having been rejected by Demetrius before the play begins, she has less self-esteem than Hermia and is comparatively timid. Her betrayal of the elopement plans to Demetrius, her undignified pursuit of him to the wood, her inability to credit that Demetrius and Lysander have fallen in love with her, and finally her lengthy appeal to Hermia to respect their childhood friendship, culminating in a call for 'pity' and an absurd forecast of her own 'death' (III.2.235 and 244), are all the actions of someone who has come to see herself as a victim. Her final lines express wonderment that she has been reunited with Demetrius, coupled with a lingering uncertainty. After all that she has been through, part of her feels he is still 'not mine own' (IV.1.191).

It is notable that the two young women do not speak at all in Act V. Some critics have speculated that they are still in shock at their treatment by their lovers, but it may simply be that they are no longer so significant to the story once they are married and that it would not be proper for young wives to join in the banter over the play.

Lysander is for the most part a model young aristocrat. He woos Hermia with poems, songs and gifts, is coolly assertive in his dealings with Egeus and his rival Demetrius, and is smoothly courteous to Theseus. In the Folio version of the text, he even assists Theseus by reading the descriptions of the proposed entertainments (see Note on the Text at the start of 'Summaries & Commentaries'). The elopement plan shows his initiative, though his inability to find his way through the wood soon takes away some of our admiration for him. Under the influence of the magic juice he becomes extremely abusive to Hermia. This is shockingly out of line with his earlier behaviour and therefore all the more amusing to the audience.

Demetrius is a less sympathetic figure. Before the play begins he has courted Helena, then abandoned her for Hermia. He is determined to marry the latter, regardless of the fact that she is in love with someone else. If he was actually 'betrothed' to Helena, as he seems to admit at IV.1.170, then it is doubtful whether a marriage to Hermia would have been legal. In Act I Scene 1 we see him ridiculed by Lysander and in Act II Scene 1 comically pursued around the stage by Helena. In Act III Scene 2 he is unpleasant to Hermia when she is distraught at the loss of Lysander. Only when the magic juice has been placed on his eyes does he show honour and dignity, and in fact he is the only one of the four lovers from whom the spell is never removed. This has worried some critics, who feel that his love for Helena is consequently a false one and that this inauthenticity detracts from the happy ending. In response, however, it has been argued that Demetrius has only been restored to his original love, the 'natural taste' of which he speaks so movingly when he awakens in the morning (IV.1.173).

The two young women remain constant in their allegiance throughout the play; it is the men whose attachments change. Despite the affection which Hermia and Helena feel for them, the two male lovers never display any originality or insight, finishing the play by making derisive comments about 'Pyramus and Thisbe,' quite unable to detect its relevance to their own experience.

THE CRAFTSMEN

The craftsmen are described patronisingly by others (to Robin they are 'hempen homespuns', III.1.70, to Philostrate 'Hard-handed men ... Which never laboured in their minds till now', V.1.72–3). When they try to use a wide vocabulary they mix up their words and their attempts to write and stage a tragedy are highly comical, all in a way calculated to amuse regular theatregoers and urban sophisticates. Nonetheless, we enjoy their struggle with the demands of drama and we admire their determination to succeed.

The craftsmen's names reflect their jobs. As a carpenter, Quince would use wooden wedges called quines or quoins. Snug the joiner would make snugly tight joints. The name of Flute the bellows-maker suggests a pipe on a bellows-powered church organ, and also a flute-like voice which is not fully broken. Snout the tinker mends the spouts (or 'snouts') of kettles. Tailors were proverbially undernourished and no doubt the expressively named Starveling was a part intended for Sincklo, the thinnest actor in Shakespeare's company. Bottom the weaver unwinds the thread from a bottom or reel. His name may also carry the sense of 'bottom' as 'the sitting part of the body,' which might then tie in neatly with his later transformation into an 'ass'. While it is not certain that either of these words had their modern vulgar meaning in Shakespeare's day, a play of 1599, *The Shoemaker's Holiday* by Thomas Dekker, includes the name 'Mistress Frigbottom' and Shakespeare's use of the word 'ass' (for example, *Hamlet* II.2.395) does sometimes sound suspiciously as if it has its modern association, punning on the long-established word which was written in Chaucer's fourteenth-century *Miller's Tale* as 'ers'.

Most of the craftsmen receive little individual character development. We know that Francis Flute is the youngest, his voice unbroken, his beard still 'coming' (I.2.44) and for these reasons he is assigned the role of Thisbe. Snug is 'slow of study' (I.2.63) so is made the lion, a role with no (or, as it turns out, just a few) lines. Tom Snout is originally cast as Thisbe's father, then switched to the somewhat limited role of a wall. Similarly, Robin Starveling is switched from playing Thisbe's mother to Moonshine, where he is put out by heckling and fails to deliver all of his speech. All four men look for guidance to Peter Quince, who seems to be not only the director, but also the author of 'Pyramus and Thisbe'. Since there is no record of classical plays being acted by workers, Quince is certainly original in his ideas and he behaves throughout as the leader of the project, assigning the parts, taking on the rewriting, directing the rehearsals and, not least among his achievements, flattering Bottom into co-operation. His speech is always decisive in tone, until he is before the audience at the palace, where he suffers a loss of nerve and delivers his lines badly in the role of Prologue.

BOTTOM

Nick Bottom is called by the puck 'the shallowest thickskin of that barren sort' (III.2.13), but he is always full of ideas and enthusiasm, and it is his bumptious self-confidence as much as Quince's powers of organisation which carries the play through rehearsals and performance. Without him, the others simply give up. They call him 'Bully,' a friendly and appreciative term. He shares something of the exuberance of the puck and, like him, aspires to take on different identities (a woman, a lion and, best of all, a tyrant who rants and swaggers, 'a part to tear a cat in', I.2.26). Whereas the puck is able to call upon supernatural powers to become a foal, a stool and so on, Bottom has to be content with what can be done by mere acting – at least until the puck lends him a hand with his magic spells. Fortunately, Bottom is too thick-skinned to notice how bad an actor he is. His insensitivity in fact proves to be his salvation. Even when equipped with an ass's head and propositioned by the queen of the fairies, he is not seriously alarmed or even curious about what has happened to him, but gets on with playing with relish the part in which he finds himself. In his dealings with the fairies, he is not at all self-conscious about mimicking courtly speech and manners. Indeed he manages to be considerably more civilised than the real aristocrats who jeer at his play in Act V. Since it is likely that the fairies would have originally been played by children, his kindly, slightly patronising treatment of them would probably have been seen in a positive light by the audience.

When restored to his normal self, Bottom struggles to find words for his bizarre experiences, but is not overcome by them and is soon enthusing his fellow craftsmen and acting his heart out. When his courtly audience mock him, he gives as good as he gets and wins them over. The actor who first played Bottom was probably Will Kempe, who was the star clown of Shakespeare's company from about 1594 to 1599. Kempe was famous for his dancing (after he left the Lord Chamberlain's Men, he kept his name before the public by dancing from London to Norwich), so when in Act V the craftsmen perform a bergomask dance, we have to picture not an irrelevant prance round the stage by modern actors, but a high-powered, expertly comical piece of clowning which would have brought Bottom's performance to an end on a very high note. Although we laugh at Bottom for his crude acting, insensitive self-assertion and lack of high culture, we also laugh with him because of his adaptability and his determination to keep going and succeed when a 'wiser' man would have given up.

THE FAIRIES

Traditionally, fairies had been conceived of as much more hostile figures than they are in *A Midsummer Night's Dream*. Even in Shakespeare's other plays they are mentioned as creatures which torment mortals by pinching them. Here they are comparatively benign, though not as sweet and flimsy as they were to become in later literature. They are not from the underworld, as Christians who believed in their existence but rejected pagan superstition would logically assume, but 'spirits of another sort' (III.2.388).

Their references to India and to their speedy globetrotting convey a sense of freedom and power. Unlike the fairies of tradition, they perform neighbourly deeds without demanding payment. They do not abduct children, but instead quarrel over who is to adopt and care for the little orphan boy. Their only venture into kidnapping and bewitching is the transformation of Bottom, who is fed, flattered and restored unharmed, without having a limb lopped off or his sanity destroyed as was the traditional fairy practice. Far from deliberately hurting people, they show guilt about their influence on the weather and eagerly bless the triple wedding. Such wicked fairy deeds as are mentioned in the play are attributed to the puck alone, who is not an evil spirit, merely 'shrewd and knavish' (II.1.33), and is kept on a tight rein by the king, Oberon.

Titania and Puck seem to be the same size as humans – Titania can take Bottom in her arms. Their attendants, who are able to hide inside flowers and fight bees, are much smaller and this would presumably have been approximated by using child actors – though if and when children were not available, the actors playing Snout, Snug, Flute and Starveling could conveniently have doubled the parts. Titania's four attendants are named after natural medicines. Cobwebs were placed on cuts to staunch blood. Mustardseed was used in a poultice to relieve stiff muscles. Part of the pea plant could be used as an ointment against the pain of lost love. Boiled moths were an ingredient of various plasters and potions.

The fairies embody the forces of nature. The effect of this **personification** is to make the cosmos seem a place which, though it may be unpredictable and sometimes dangerous, is ultimately friendly to the human species, even similar in its structure to Elizabethan society. However, like all elements of the play, there is a reverse side to this conception. The audience never forgets that the world of the fairies is a comic device. We enjoy seeing a 'humanised' version of nature, but we know that the real world of nature is not like this.

OBERON

Oberon has natural authority. His speech is always decisive and imperative, and he is used to getting his way. He may strike a modern audience, familiar with ideals of democracy and equality, as a slightly sinister figure. In particular, we may suspect his motives in wanting the little boy for his 'bower' (IV.1.60). However, it can be argued that Titania is holding back the child from his natural growth into manhood, crowning him with flowers when he should be taking on the masculine role of knight. Like other key elements of the play, the character of

Oberon has two sides to it, of which we see first one, then the other. He is swift in his mood changes, fiercely jealous, then forgiving. However, he is not human, but a mythical figure, embodying Elizabethan ideas of masculinity, and he does make a consistent effort to help Helena and the others, taking pity on her as 'a sweet Athenian lady' (II.1.260) and intervening three times through Robin until she finally gets her love. Oberon has supernatural powers, being able to see further into the heavens than Robin, understand the power of the magic juice, and in the last scene cast a protective spell over unborn children. In his speeches he is capable of a descriptive beauty beyond that achieved by the mortal characters.

TITANIA
Titania is like Oberon in many respects. She too is authoritative, well-intentioned towards the mortals and capable of speaking in memorably poetic lines. Although she is seen to be caring and maternal in her attitude towards her votaress and 'young squire' (II.1.131), and towards the human beings harmed by the unseasonable weather, under the influence of the magic juice she does show a more possessive side to her nature, caring for Bottom indeed but also taking him prisoner with the words, 'Thou shalt remain here, whether thou wilt or no' (III.1.144). Shakespeare seems to assume that, as an embodiment of natural femininity, she must inevitably submit to her husband's will in the end. However, she is by no means easily dominated. Her name seems to have come from Ovid's *Metamorphoses*, where it is a synonym for the goddess Diana.

THE PUCK
Shakespeare sets him down in the original stage directions as 'Robin', 'Rob' or 'Puck'. Most editions of the play have adopted 'Puck' as a general title for him, but that is not his name. His name is Robin and he is *a* puck, a kind of goblin. He is not a fairy; the fairy in Act II Scene 1 certainly recognises him as different from herself. Before Shakespeare, he was not classified as a puck either, but as an earth spirit. In folklore he always carried a broom with him (as he seems to do in Act V, when he tells us 'I am sent with broom before', V.1.379) so that he could help maids who had behaved well and so deserved his assistance. He also took

a great interest in sorting out love conflicts, as in a fashion he does in *A Midsummer Night's Dream*.

His last name, Goodfellow, is a propitiatory coinage, given to him by countryfolk who wish to flatter him into leaving them alone. He delights in mischief and is enjoyed by the audience as one who brings fun, which he does without offending our conscience and our sense of identification with the victims. With one exception (the fairy in Act II Scene 1), he speaks only to Oberon and the audience, with the result that he seems almost to exist outside the rest of the drama, unconstrained by the actions and expectations of others. To some extent, the puck is our representative, carrying out the mischief we hope to enjoy, commenting on it and addressing us directly at the end. He is free to use a wide range of **verse** forms, **couplets** of various lengths and **quatrains** as well as **blank verse**, and he employs a wide range of tones. Where Bottom aspires to play the hero, the love interest and the lion, the puck can actually become a foal, a crab, a stool, a horse, a dog, a hog, a bear and even a fire, but to a still greater degree than Bottom he is unaffected by his experiences and always remains himself. Where the marriages change the mortals who undertake them as a pivotal part of their journey through life to death, the spirits are immortal, immaterial and incapable of development.

LANGUAGE & STYLE

As in all Shakespeare's plays, the characters largely speak in **blank verse**, with rhyming **couplets** used to mark an exit or the end of a scene. Because many lines are **end-stopped**, placing emphasis on the final word, it is easy for both the Athenian nobles and the fairies to move from blank verse into couplets or some other rhyme scheme. The extra rhyming can have a variety of functions. At the end of the opening scene, for example, it serves to distance us from the lovers' experience; in Act II Scene 2 and Act III Scene 2 it makes the male lovers' declarations seem stilted and pompous; in Act III Scene 1 it points up the contrast between the exotic Titania and the prosaic Bottom.

The fairies make particular use of rhyme when uttering spells and charms or carrying out supernatural actions. All of their short-lined passages are rhymed, giving them a chanted, song-like quality. The fairies' lullaby for Titania in Act II Scene 2 is an actual song and it is possible that some of the other passages were also meant to be sung, especially the various spells, and perhaps even the lines which are uttered by Robin, Oberon and Titania before their departure in Act IV Scene 1. The fairies' final blessing in Act V Scene 1 entails singing and dancing, but the text as we have it does not seem to contain the words they sing, unless we consider that lines 381–90 should themselves be set to music – which (with lines 411–12 added at the end) was the solution adopted by Mendelssohn.

Its highly patterned **plot** and many theatrical effects make the play a particularly suitable one for music. Even in Shakespeare's lifetime music seems to have been added at the end of Act III (see 'Critical History & Broader Perspectives'), Purcell soon turned the play into an opera and Mendelssohn produced an outstanding accompaniment in his *Overture* and *Incidental Music*. Duke Ellington's Shakespearean jazz album, *Such Sweet Thunder*, includes the composition 'Up and Down, Up and Down (I Will Lead Them Up and Down)' in which pairs of musicians take the roles of the couples in the wood and the trumpet imitates the intonation of the puck. Benjamin Britten's highly successful opera continued the tradition into the 1960s.

Decades earlier, Bernard Shaw had pointed out that the play is 'operatic' in its very nature with duets between characters, as they combine to create a mood and share ideas: for example, Theseus and Hippolyta's debate about the moon in the opening eleven lines, Lysander and Hermia's lament for the fate of lovers (I.1.132–55), or Robin and Oberon's conversation about spirits and the dawn (III.2.378–93). There are also 'arias' for individual characters, speeches where the action seems to stand still for passages of conspicuous beauty: among them, Titania's 'These are the forgeries of jealousy' (II.1.81–117), Oberon's 'I know a bank where the wild thyme blows' (II.1.249–56), and Helena's 'We, Hermia, like two artificial gods' (III.2.203–19).

The craftsmen vary the tone and rhythm of the play by speaking in **prose** – although Bottom still manages his own kind of 'aria' at the end of Act IV Scene 1 – except in their dire efforts to perform in rhyming **verse**, which parody the techniques Shakespeare uses so brilliantly elsewhere. Short, rhymed lines and **alliteration** fail conspicuously in

'Pyramus and Thisbe' because the formal patterning and the meaning are so at odds with each other.

Lists are a common feature of the play, as Shakespeare works to create the details of new worlds in our imagination. Egeus lists the love tokens bestowed on his daughter. Oberon lists the beasts with which Titania might fall in love. Hermia and Lysander list the obstacles to love. The fairies offer Bottom a list of gifts.

'Therefore' is a particularly favoured conjunction, as the characters rationalise their way through the fantastic events by insisting on logical connections between them, sometimes persuasively, sometimes not. When we hear that Theseus can see through 'saucy and audacious eloquence', 'therefore' he appreciates what is genuine (V.1.103–4), and that Oberon, seeing a fight is about to begin, 'therefore' sends Robin to prevent it (III.2.355), it is hard to fault their logic. Demetrius's argument to Helena, 'I love thee not, therefore pursue me not', is equally logical, but futile in the context of her passion (II.1.188). Titania's assertions that she has quarrelled with Oberon, 'therefore' the winds and the moon have reacted angrily, is beyond our understanding, although we accept it for the sake of the play (II.1.103). Snout's view that Snug dressed as a lion will terrify the audience, 'therefore' there should be a prologue on the subject, is less than convincing (III.1.31). Lysander's statement to Hermia that he agrees they should patiently bear their affliction, 'therefore' they should elope, makes no sense at all, but we happily accede to it, as does she (I.1.156).

Overall, we may say that the language of the play is always forming beautiful patterns, but that their relation to the 'real world' is never clear, for the focus of the play is not so much on objective reality as on the characters' changing perceptions of it.

IMAGERY & SYMBOLISM

Only one scene of the play (Act IV Scene 1) takes place in the clear light of day. As its title implies, the rest of *A Midsummer Night's Dream* is set at night or indoors. Before the invention of street-lighting, natural darkness was a much more common experience than it is today, and Shakespeare's original audience would have readily conceived of a moonlit wood as a place where people were out of their element, blundering and apprehensive – a highly suitable place to explore the mysteries of love and nature, since these may also, in their own way, leave us unsure of our ground.

Elizabethan plays were acted in daylight, or indoors by the light of flaming torches – in either case, with little or no scenery (see Shakespeare's Theatre) – so speech had to be used to evoke scenic detail in the imaginations of the audience. In the case of *A Midsummer Night's Dream* repeated references to the moon conjure up in the mind's eye a mysterious, gentle light which transforms everything upon which it falls. However, the lunar references have more significance than the establishment of a magical atmosphere, important though that may be. The moon is also used to suggest a range of ideas which are of thematic relevance to the play.

There was a long-standing belief still current in Elizabethan times that, while the heavens were as God had created them, perfect and unchanging, the fall of man had made the area from the moon down to the earth – the 'sublunary' world – imperfect and unstable. Hence change, decay and death could not be avoided in our world, and earthly love, in contrast to divine love, would often prove unreliable and impermanent. In Act II Scene 2 of *Romeo and Juliet*, Juliet cautions Romeo against swearing by the 'inconstant moon / That monthly changes in her circled orb'. As a symbol of inconstancy and imperfection, the moon is clearly relevant to the rapidly changing allegiances of Demetrius and Lysander. As the 'governess of floods' (II.1.103), the changing moon has a mysterious rhythmic affinity, not only with the tides, but with the female fertility cycle, and it can be associated with other cyclic and broadly predictable changes like the succeeding of the generations.

In a sense the whole play runs to lunar time. Lysander has charmed Hermia by moonlight and sets the time of their elopement by the moon, Theseus and Hippolyta reckon the time to their marriage by the moon's phases, Titania's fairy and Oberon measure their speed against the moon, Hermia measures her incredulity against the likelihood of the moon passing through the centre of the earth, Quince arranges his rehearsals for moonlight, and Pyramus cannot die until the moon has sympathetically withdrawn from the stage. Although characters constantly refer to the moon, the nature of that moon is inconsistent, changing, like love, with the eye of the beholder. Theseus confidently announces in Act I Scene 1 that the new moon will not be seen until his wedding to Hippolyta in four days' time, but the moon seems to be shining brightly that very night and the wedding itself arrives in a mere two days. It is true that Shakespeare often disregards such minor details of continuity which are unlikely to be noticed in theatrical performance, but it is also true that the moonlit world of Acts II to IV is deeply disorientating and irrational. We could not expect anything else, since lunacy is by definition 'a state brought on by the moon' and in Elizabethan English 'wood' could mean maddened, as it does for the exasperated Demetrius at II.1.192.

Several critics have suggested that Hippolyta's opening reference to 'the moon – like to a silver bow' (I.1.9), an **image** likely enough to occur to a bow-carrying Amazon, would also suggest to an educated Elizabethan the image of Diana, the goddess of hunting and of chastity. 'Dian's bud' (IV.1.72) is the apt name which Oberon gives the antidote to the magic juice. Diana was generally identified with the moon goddess Phoebe (I.1.209), as she is by Theseus when he warns Hermia that as a celibate nun at 'Diana's altar' (I.1.89) she would have to chant hymns to 'the cold fruitless moon' (I.1.73). Oberon later associates them again when he speaks of Elizabeth, the Virgin Queen, being defended by 'the chaste beams of the watery moon' (II.1.162).

Although chastity has to be spoken of with respect when it is associated with the Queen of England, the play's preferred goal is marriage and it pointedly opens by celebrating a defeat of chastity: Theseus's martial and marital victories over Hippolyta, Queen of the celibate Amazons. Hippolyta's image of a bow ready to fire calls to mind not only Diana, but Cupid, who is mentioned not long after by Helena (I.1.235). Paradoxically, Diana herself is the goddess of fertility as well as chastity.

All this seems complicated, and perhaps is, but fortunately the play does not spell out these matters or expect us to reflect upon them explicitly. The moon is simply a **symbol** with several associations – madness, chastity and fertility – all of which are relevant to the **themes** of the play. The moon's presence evokes these three states, but it is left to the characters to experience them and to the audience to decide how they may be linked.

A Midsummer Night's Dream refers to the moon more frequently than does any other Shakespeare play. The same applies to a second key **image**: that of eyes. Eyes are associated with sexual attraction, both for how they appear and for what they see. Helena's plea to Hermia, 'O, teach me how you look' (I.1.192) forcefully combines both meanings. Eyes are also associated with subjectivity. The wood at night is a place where eyes cannot operate as effectively as their owners would like – darkness 'from the eye his function takes' and 'doth impair the seeing sense' (III.2.177–9) – so that the encounters in the wood become representative of the encounters of love in general, where what we feel about someone is more important than the simple facts of what we see. As Helena puts it, 'Love looks not with the eyes, but with the mind, / And therefore is winged Cupid painted blind' (I.1.234–5). Reversing the process, it is to the eyes that the magic juice is applied, changing perception and, by so doing, changing feeling. Confronted by Lysander's altered allegiance, Hermia threatens to retaliate by scratching out Helena's offending eyes.

The effect of the magic juice is to speed up the process of falling in and out of love so that it comes to seem absurd. Nonetheless, while we are invited to laugh at the lovers, we are not expected to condemn them. It is part of the human condition that the inner world of our feelings and the outer world of external facts can be difficult to bring into harmony or even to speak about meaningfully. This uncertain relationship between what our senses detect and what our minds make of it is comically reflected in Quince's clumsy description of how Pyramus goes 'but to see a noise that he heard' (III.1.84) and Bottom's efforts when playing Pyramus to 'hear … Thisbe's face' (V.1.190). Such sensory dislocation is carried to an extreme when Bottom attempts to formulate his experiences in the wood at night: 'The eye of man hath not heard, the ear of man hath not seen, man's hand is not able to taste, his tongue to conceive, nor his heart to report what my dream was!' (IV.1.208–11).

Some critics (notably Paul Olson in his essay, 'The Meaning of Court Marriage', 1957, see Price 1983, in Critical History & Broader Perspectives) have argued that the play presents us with two kinds of love: the superficial physical attractions of the eye, represented by the magic juice, and the settled, mature affection of the mind. However, it is difficult to reconcile this simple opposition with the example of

Demetrius, whose settled affection comes about precisely from the application of the juice. Ultimately, *A Midsummer Night's Dream* is a play, not a treatise on the subject–object relation. It does not attempt to solve such philosophical questions, only to acknowledge that the nature of our own feelings can be a mystery to us and that we are, to a degree, driven by forces beyond our comprehension and control.

Before the rise of science, one of the main ways of coming to terms with such forces was mythology: stories of gods and other supernatural beings whose deeds created the world which we inhabit today. *A Midsummer Night's Dream* supplies us with a parody of mythology in the shape of the fairies and also contains many references to figures from classical mythology, as suits its setting in ancient Athens. References to, for example, the Fates, the Furies and Venus reinforce the impression of humans impelled by forces beyond their grasp. However, since the setting of the play shares some of the features of classical Greece and Elizabethan England, these learned and exotic references are balanced by homegrown images of English beasts, flowers and birds: 'a fat and bean-fed horse' (II.1.45), 'oxlips and the nodding violet' (II.1.250) and 'russet-pated choughs' (III.2.21).

Like a science fiction story, *A Midsummer Night's Dream* is set somewhere which is both like and unlike our own reality. Its world is both ancient Athens and Elizabethan England, night and day, common experience and fantastic dream. We are invited to enjoy its colourful differences to our own world, but also to think about any revealing similarities.

THEMES

LOVE

Traditionally, a **comedy** is a play about two lovers whose path to marriage is blocked by members of the older generation, but who eventually, after a series of entertaining **plot** devices, succeed in getting the upper hand and marrying after all. In his earlier comedies Shakespeare had shown a liking for making the traditional comic situations still more farcical by bringing onto the stage not simply two lovers but two or more pairs of them, and even making some of them identical twins. One objection to this approach is that placing so much emphasis on elaborate plot development can make the portrayal of love shallow and unconvincing. Towards the end of *The Two Gentlemen of Verona*, for example, Valentine decides to make a gift of the woman he loves, Silvia, to his old friend Proteus, even though Proteus has tried to rape her a few moments before. This provides an interesting twist to the plot, but in doing so damages the characterisation beyond repair. In *A Midsummer Night's Dream*, however, Shakespeare converts the potential defect into an advantage. He puts the irrationality of love at the very centre of the play and makes it one of its chief subjects.

The basic comic plot of a father (Egeus) attempting to thwart a young couple (Hermia and Lysander) is developed in comparatively routine fashion, so much so that its resolution is accomplished in one line: 'Egeus, I will overbear your will' (IV.1.178). However, the love plot is such an accepted theatrical device and so powerful in its appeal, that it survives this, just as it survives the introduction of a second couple, Helena and Demetrius (indeed three more couples, if we also count Theseus and Hippolyta and Oberon and Titania). The acts of courtship between Lysander and Hermia which Egeus dismisses as 'feigning' (I.1.31) are accepted by the audience as signs of emotional commitment, and we are moved by the couple's willingness to die rather than live parted. Hermia, in particular, is ready to risk execution or a lifetime imprisoned in a convent. Both partners are aware that lovers before them have come to sad ends, and the story of Pyramus and Thisbe, however ineptly executed by the craftsmen, reminds us that love can be a source of tragedy as easily as of comedy. Its striking similarity to the story of Romeo and Juliet is a reminder that if Egeus had got his way, Lysander and Hermia might have similarly ended by killing themselves in despair.

However, although *A Midsummer Night's Dream* offers us a glimpse of the tragic view of love seen in *Romeo and Juliet*, the emphasis adopted on this occasion proves to be a very different one. The love interest with which the play opens is soon modified by Helena's soliloquy at the end of Act I Scene 1, which highlights not so much the overwhelming importance of love as its subjective, irrational nature. In Acts II and III the intervention of Oberon and Robin with their magic juice speeds up the process of falling in and out of love in a way which makes it highly comical. The lovers' speeches which try to explain and justify their love as rational and consistent with their normal thinking only serve to make them seem more absurd in their behaviour. As in Shakespeare's other plays and his **sonnets**, love is depicted as a kind of benign affliction, which can exist in contradiction to one's normal feelings and ideas, and which can sometimes lead us to do things which are foolish or hurtful. Love's reverse side is jealousy. While the audience are joining in with Robin's laughter at the folly of the mortals, Lysander and Demetrius are trying to kill one another, and Helena and Hermia are suffering from the rejection, with considerable verbal abuse, which they have received from the men whom they love.

But in the end love is not denied. Hermia has her Lysander, Helena has her Demetrius, and, for that matter, Theseus has his Hippolyta, and Oberon his Titania – though, like the younger lovers, the two older couples experience serious difficulties along the way, Theseus and Hippolyta making war against each other before the play begins, and Oberon and Titania becoming temporarily estranged by their quarrel.

We must not forget the fifth couple, who make the oddest pairing of all. Titania and Bottom share the shortest time together, but it is long enough to demonstrate the extremes of love's irrationality. When Titania embraces Bottom, Shakespeare seems to be telling us that sexual attraction is not only arbitrary, but liable by its nature to sometimes take forms which are unsustainable or which society finds perverse. A similar point is made in the sonnets, written around this time, in which the poet, who finds himself fixated both upon a lady as unfashionably dark as Hermia and upon a man as disloyal as Demetrius, can only exclaim, 'O me! what eyes hath Love put in my head, / Which have no correspondence with true sight … ?' (Sonnet 148).

MARRIAGE

Shakespeare was much influenced in this play by Ovid's *Metamorphoses*, a book of tales of supernatural transformation (see Literary Background). Unlike the changes portrayed by Ovid, however, the ones he depicts in *A Midsummer Night's Dream* are not predominantly arbitrary supernatural acts. The changes which do fit that description are the short-term **plot** devices such as the ass's head and the magic juice. The major transformations – from rehearsal to performance, from child to adult, from single person to couple – each involve a permanent growth from one state to the next.

A Midsummer Night's Dream consistently takes apparent oppositions and demonstrates either that they are natural stages in such a process (youth and age, celibacy and sex, singleness and marriage) or that they are mutually supportive pairs (day and night, male and female, wakefulness and dreaming, actor and audience, city and wood, reason and imagination). Each side of these pairs has its own positive and negative aspects. The forest is both threatening and supportive; celibacy is both 'blessèd' and a 'withering' of life (I.1.74–7); Bottom is both an idiot and a hero; Theseus is both a wise ruler and a man of limited imagination.

The play does not suggest that one aspect or term is right and its opposite wrong, but seeks to marry them together to create something greater than either. In the case of eight of the characters it does so literally by marriage. *A Midsummer Night's Dream* is thematically a marriage play, whether or not it was written to celebrate a particular wedding. Marriage takes what might seem opposites – two people with separate experiences and aspirations – and reveals them to be potentially complementary to each other, creating something greater than the two were separately.

Like humans, the elements can be in harmony or at odds, and the presence of Oberon and Titania implies that love between people is equivalent to, or an actual form of, the divine force which powers the cosmos. Love, as we still say, makes the world go round. By setting his play in ancient Athens, Shakespeare avoids any clumsily blasphemous reference to religion, but the whole apparatus of the fairy world is substituted for the mythological and religious frames of reference which human beings have devised to make sense of the world they inhabit.

Appropriately, given its preoccupation with marriage and the movement from generation to generation, the play is shaped by the fertility rituals of Maying. May Day, when the countryside moves from spring to summer, was naturally a time when people's thoughts turned to the fertility of the land and of their own species. Countryfolk danced round the phallic **symbol** of the 'painted maypole' (to which Hermia insultingly compares Helena at III.2.296) and went out into woods and hills while it was still night to have fun together and bring home branches for festive decoration, as Lysander reminds Hermia that they had once done with Helena (I.1.166–7). Such excursions provided an ideal opportunity for the young people to choose their life-partners without the intervention of their elders and, as horrified Puritans pointed out, to engage in pre-marital sex. Scholars have argued that historically all comedy has its roots in fertility ceremonies, and *A Midsummer Night's Dream* certainly supports the case. Like initiates in a coming-of-age rite, the four lovers leave the city and their rationally ordered, comprehensible daytime world and, entering the wood, pass through a night of irrational, dream-like experiences which transforms them from disobedient children into adults accepted by society and partnered in marriage, ready now to become parents themselves.

The shift of location between city and country is a favourite device in Shakespeare's comedies. A similar movement from the normal world to a **pastoral** one and back again also occurs in *The Two Gentlemen of Verona* and *As You Like It*, and there are comparable excursions in other plays like *The Merchant of Venice* and *The Winter's Tale*. In this case, the play begins and ends in Athens, a city famous for the reasoning powers of its great thinkers, Socrates, Plato and Aristotle; then, in total contrast, the long central section of the play spanning Acts II to IV, takes us to a wood outside the city's bounds, where human laws and reasoning virtually cease to apply. The rational, man-made world which rules the day and the non-rational, spontaneous world of dreams are both part of our experience; both are required when we pass through the great turning points and crises of our lives; both are involved in the creation of art.

GENDER

The transformations in the play which have attracted most attention in recent years have been those connected with gender. To some degree the play seems to be an assertion of male authority. Robin Goodfellow intends to reassure us when he says:

> Jack shall have Jill;
> Naught shall go ill.
> The man shall have his mare again, and all shall be well. (III.2.461–3)

Today, however, his apparent equation of woman with animal property is more likely to give offence than reassurance. Worse still, the playwright

puts similar sentiments into the mouth of Helena, who comically
compares herself and Hermia to a spaniel (II.1.203), a bear (II.2.100) and
a vixen (III.2.324).

The play is certainly not feminist in its assumptions. This is hardly
surprising, given the social position of women in the sixteenth century.
Moreover, it is a play by a male author and in the original production the
female parts would have been played by men. The drama begins with
Theseus speaking of how he conquered the female society of the
Amazons by force. Later Oberon conquers Titania by a hideous trick,
while Lysander and Demetrius desert, insult and threaten the women
who love them – events which the audience are expected to find
humorous. Hermia and Helena do achieve the husbands they desire, but
only because the authority of Oberon and Theseus, greater male power
figures, overrules that of Egeus. Once Hermia and Helena are married
and in their role as wives, they cease to contribute any dialogue. Their
marriages are finally blessed by the most authoritative male in the play,
Oberon. In keeping with this emphasis on male authority, mention is
made of the young women's fathers, Egeus and Nedar, but not their
mothers. The only mother referred to in the whole play is the 'votaress'
who dies before the drama has begun.

Male and female are so opposed in the play that even the accounts
of the 'changeling boy' are biased by gender, Robin stating that the child
was stolen from an Indian king, Titania that his mother left him an
orphan. Titania's attachment to the boy actually seems less motivated by
affection for him than by love for his late mother. She speaks of how the
two women shared the experience of the votaress's pregnancy and
mocked the merchant ships, symbols of male authority. Such all-female
groupings are portrayed as happy ones, but not allowed to persist.
Hippolyta has to leave her fellow Amazons, and although Helena
reminds Hermia of their loving girlhood together, her nostalgic picture
of their pre-adolescent happiness is soon dispelled by their quarrels over
men.

Yet, substantial as the play's gender bias may be, we should not
overstate it. The play celebrates marriage, not male dominance, even if
the male is conceived of as the superior partner. Titania's rebellion against
her husband is portrayed sympathetically, as is Hermia's rebellion against
her father. When Theseus tells Hermia, 'To you your father should be as

a god' (I.1.47), the audience are unlikely to share his opinion of that blustering personage, and the play contains many examples of laughable behaviour by male figures, including Oberon. Oberon's own reference to Queen Elizabeth (II.1.158) reminds us that this largely male-dominated society was ruled by a powerful and respected Queen. While it may be true that the play depicts male superiority as more 'natural' than female superiority, it also offers us many female points of view and shows males and females interacting with each other in a variety of ways, with the females often highly sympathetic and assertive. Marriage in the play is depicted not as a closed institution with a simple set of rules which must be followed, but as a dynamic relationship which has constantly to be negotiated afresh.

THEATRE

A Midsummer Night's Dream is a play which flaunts its own theatricality. We are required to 'believe' that any number of things are happening before our eyes when plainly they are not. Not only can the stage be a palace in one scene and a wood in the next, but it can become several parts of the wood at once. Assured that Oberon is invisible and Cobweb tiny enough to take on a bee in single combat, we behave rather like the lovers with the juice on their eyes and see what we are told to see – and we do so despite Shakespeare's repeatedly drawing our attention to the trick. When, for example, Quince points at the stage and says, 'This green plot shall be our stage' (III.1.3), we find ourselves thinking of the stage as a green plot, then as a stage, then as a green plot again, while all the time our eyes literally see a stage. When Francis Flute resists being cast as a woman and later when he appears as Thisbe, we are reminded that Hippolyta, Hermia, Helena and Titania were not played by women when Shakespeare's play was first staged, but by highly talented young men in 'drag'.

Each appearance by Peter Quince and his company of amateur actors is a reminder to us that any play is constructed with difficulty, and requires not only skilful acting if it is to succeed, but a sympathetic audience ready to pay it the right kind of attention. In the case of 'Pyramus and Thisbe' an audience full of 'self affairs' and actors who lack skill impede the performance. Even so, Hippolyta has to confess that she cannot resist Bottom's tragic turn: 'Beshrew my heart, but I pity the man' (V.1.282). In the contrasting case of *A Midsummer Night's Dream*, the audience constantly attains that mixed state of awareness, a kind of waking dreaming, which allows them to see what is literally before their eyes and, at the same time, what the playwright wishes it to represent.

One effect of repeatedly drawing our attention to the artificiality of the play is to show that it is more than a simple imitation of reality. We might think that only naïve performers like Quince and company could believe that the audience will mistake their acting for 'real life' and so panic at the entry of a bumpkin in a lion costume. But Theseus too makes the same mistake when he says of actors, 'The best in this kind are but shadows' (V.1.208). Since a shadow has no purpose in its own right and conveys only a vague, passive impression of the person or thing which has thrown it, a play made of shadows can be nothing more than a rough impression of the kinds of things which happen in real life. If such realism had been Shakespeare's goal in *A Midsummer Night's Dream*, surely his play would not have contained fairies, invisibility, magic juice, a man with the head of an ass and characters from ancient legends such as Theseus himself.

In the epilogue (V.1.413) Robin revives the expression 'shadows', but in a way which challenges Theseus's use of it. The puck's phrase 'we shadows' seems at first to refer to himself and the fairies as nocturnal creatures (echoing his earlier address to Oberon as 'King of shadows', III.2.347), but soon comes to be understood as a reference to the acting company also. In what sense, then, are we to take his use of the expression 'shadows'? Is the actor playing Robin conceding that he and his colleagues are crude imitators of real life like Peter Quince? Or is he identifying the actors with some of the qualities of the fairies – dream-like creatures who first observe the mortal world from a distance, then intervene in it ('I'll be an auditor – An actor too, perhaps, if I see cause', III.1.72–3)? Or is his position somewhere between the two, hinting that a play is both an imitation of life and a creative transformation of it which draws upon those imaginative aspects of the mind which are revealed during dreams?

The epilogue does not furnish an answer, but invites the audience to reach their own verdict. Unlike the characters, we are able to see and interpret the overall dramatic pattern. In this, of course, we are in a similar position to the Athenian aristocrats when they watch 'Pyramus and Thisbe'. For their part, they complacently believe themselves to be spectators at a silly diversion which has no relevance to their own lives. We, however, know from our superior vantage point that the Athenian lovers have been in as potentially tragic a situation as Pyramus and Thisbe and that to some degree their own behaviour has been scripted by forces whose existence they deny: the fairies.

Could any of this have an application to us? Are we insulated from the world of the play, on the other side of the stage, in the 'real life' of which art is an imitation; or are we also in some sense characters following a script? We are certainly not characters in a Shakespeare play, speaking in beautiful verse, nor are we controlled by invisible fairies, but it can be argued that our lives too are shaped by forces beyond our control. Some people may, like the Elizabethans, locate such forces in the stars or divine predestination, others refer to genetic disposition, statistical probability or social conditioning, but the effect is the same. 'All the world's a stage, / And all the men and women merely players' (*As You Like It*, II.7.140–1).

Even love is not exempt from that claim, the lover being one of the roles which Jaques (from *As You Like It*) in his famous speech claims that everyone plays at some point in life. Like the illusions of drama, love is a kind of unspoken contract which can only function when others accept it. For most of this play, Helena is like a frustrated playwright or actor who cannot get others, particularly Demetrius, to take part in her script. Marriage, which in the end releases her from this frustration, is a drama-like ritual involving the adoption of a new identity before an audience.

Because *A Midsummer Night's Dream* does not emphasise explicit discussions about life and art, it is easy to mistake it for a lightweight entertainment. It does something much more skilful and satisfying, however, by integrating such ideas into the action, so that we see for ourselves the similarities between theatre and other human experience, and ourselves become part of the theatrical process. Through a kind of shared dream, mixing common experience and fantasy, Shakespeare creates worlds which parallel those normally experienced by the audience, celebrating, challenging, mocking and enriching the lives of anyone prepared to share what the epilogue calls 'these visions'.

PART FOUR

EXTENDED COMMENTARIES

TEXT 1 (II.2.94–162)

HELENA:

O, I am out of breath in this fond chase.
The more my prayer, the lesser is my grace.
Happy is Hermia, wheresoe'er she lies,
For she hath blessèd and attractive eyes.
How came her eyes so bright? Not with salt tears –
If so, my eyes are oftener washed than hers.
No, no – I am as ugly as a bear;
For beasts that meet me run away for fear.
Therefore no marvel though Demetrius
Do as a monster fly my presence thus.
What wicked and dissembling glass of mine
Made me compare with Hermia's sphery eyne?
But who is here? – Lysander on the ground?
Dead – or asleep? I see no blood, no wound.
Lysander, if you live, good sir, awake!

LYSANDER (*wakes*):

And run through fire I will for thy sweet sake!
Transparent Helena, nature shows art
That through thy bosom makes me see thy heart.
Where is Demetrius? O, how fit a word
Is that vile name to perish on my sword!

HELENA:

Do not say so, Lysander, say not so.
What though he love your Hermia, lord, what though?
Yet Hermia still loves you. Then be content.

LYSANDER:

Content with Hermia? No, I do repent
The tedious minutes I with her have spent.
Not Hermia but Helena I love.

Who will not change a raven for a dove?
The will of man is by his reason swayed,
And reason says you are the worthier maid.
Things growing are not ripe until their season;
So I, being young, till now ripe not to reason.
And touching now the point of human skill,
Reason becomes the marshal to my will,
And leads me to your eyes, where I o'erlook
Love's stories written in love's richest book.

HELENA:

Wherefore was I to this keen mockery born?
When at your hands did I deserve this scorn?
Is't not enough, is't not enough young man
That I did never – no, nor never can –
Deserve a sweet look from Demetrius' eye
But you must flout my insufficiency?
Good troth, you do me wrong – good sooth, you do –
In such disdainful manner me to woo.
But fare you well. Perforce I must confess
I thought you lord of more true gentleness.
O, that a lady of one man refused
Should of another be therefore abused!   *Exit*

LYSANDER:

She sees not Hermia. Hermia, sleep thou there,
And never mayst thou come Lysander near.
For, as a surfeit of the sweetest things
The deeper loathing to the stomach brings,
Or as the heresies that men do leave
Are hated most of those they did deceive,
So thou, my surfeit and my heresy,
Of all be hated, but the most of me!
And, all my powers, address your love and might
To honour Helen and to be her knight.   *Exit*

HERMIA (*wakes*):
Help me, Lysander, help me! Do thy best
To pluck this crawling serpent from my breast!

> Ay me, for pity! – What a dream was here!
> Lysander, look how I do quake with fear!
> Methought a serpent ate my heart away,
> And you sat smiling at his cruel prey.
> Lysander – what, removed? Lysander, lord!
> What, out of hearing? Gone? No sound, no word?
> Alack, where are you? Speak an if you hear.
> Speak, of all loves! I swoon almost with fear.
> No? Then I well perceive you are not nigh.
> Either death or you I'll find immediately.   *Exit*

We have previously witnessed Demetrius's increasingly blunt attempts to repel Helena as she follows him through the wood and her almost masochistic responses to this rejection. She implores him:

> Use me but as your spaniel: spurn me, strike me,
> Neglect me, lose me; only give me leave,
> Unworthy as I am, to follow you. (II.1.205–7)

This is an outrageous reversal of male and female roles, as Helena herself complains in the same scene (Women 'should be wooed, and were not made to woo', line 242). In the tradition of courtly love, originating in the eleventh century but still influential in the love poetry (and perhaps to a lesser extent in the behaviour) of the Elizabethan period, the woman was a distant, idealised figure, whom the male lover pursued with flattering adoration and heroic proofs of his worth. Helena's desperate seizure of the initiative is therefore comically unladylike, and this is re-established at the beginning of the present extract, where her being 'out of breath' suggests that she enters literally chasing Demetrius across the stage. Even in our day, when gender roles are more open, the sight of Helena racing after her heart's desire, and Demetrius, a brave, young, sword-carrying nobleman, running from her as fast as he can, is an incongruous one, certain to provoke laughter from any audience.

Since Helena and Demetrius last appeared, only a few minutes previously, there have been major developments in the play. Oberon has sent Robin for the magic juice and put it on the eyes of Titania, and immediately before Helena enters Robin has also put it on the eyes of Lysander, mistaking him for Demetrius. Lysander and Hermia continue to sleep on the stage, unseen by Helena, as she abandons her pursuit of

Demetrius and stops to reflect sadly on her fate. A large part of the humour and suspense in the play, as in any drama, derives from the audience knowing significantly more than do the characters. In this case, being aware that the two sleepers are nearby and that Lysander is primed to fall in love with the next creature he sees, we can easily form a hypothesis about what is likely to happen next, and can enjoy the wait to see if we are right. This interest in the larger situation tends to undermine the personal pathos of Helena's speech, which is also undercut by its neat rhyming couplets, its equally neat antitheses ('The more my prayer, the lesser is my grace') and its occasional exaggerations ('I am as ugly as a bear'). All these devices serve to distance us from Helena's emotions and ensure that we look upon her as a figure in a comic situation, rather than empathise with her as a badly treated young woman. Her wistfully jealous remarks about eyes meanwhile serve to keep before our minds an image which recurs throughout the play. Such references to eyes suggest the subjective nature of beauty and love, a suggestion which will be amply confirmed when Lysander awakes.

Helena's discovery of the sleeping Lysander produces a series of highly explicit questions ('But who is here? Lysander on the ground? / Dead – or asleep?') which seem almost to be shared with the audience, as a character might speak in a modern Christmas pantomime. The lines are indeed not far removed from Thisbe's crude declamation, 'Asleep, my love? / What, dead, my dove?' (V.1.316–17), and the effect, again, is to distance us from Helena's feelings, so that, rather than share her alarm, we see her with the detachment necessary to enjoy what will happen next.

What happens, inevitably, is that when she urges, 'Lysander, if you live, good sir, awake!' he starts up and declares his love for her with the words, 'And run through fire I will for thy sweet sake', his first line rhyming with her previous one to form a decisive, comical reply. Lysander's instant conversion from Hermia's admirer to Helena's is all that we had hoped, or feared, a total change of mind and heart, pursued regardless of Helena's disconcerted reactions and rationalised by arguments that are tritely expressed and clearly bogus.

> The will of man is by his reason swayed,
> And reason says you are the worthier maid.

This is not, we feel, how love works. However love comes about, it is not through an act of will, following a reasoning process, and it certainly does not do so in the case of Lysander who, in trying to account for his changed feelings, is merely deceiving himself. Because we have all rationalised away the real motives of our behaviour at one time or another, we appreciate the satire. However, the main source of humour lies in seeing both Lysander and Hermia caught up in a situation beyond their control.

As in the case of a pompous man who slips on a banana skin, their discomfort is a source of amusement to those who saw the fall coming and the more outcry the victims make afterwards, the funnier the joke becomes. A man slipping on a banana skin would not be funny if he did not look self-important first and, in this case too, ironic reversal is part of the comedy. Lysander's change of heart is the more entertaining because he has professed his love for Hermia so often. Similarly, Helena has just been lamenting that she is too ugly to be loved when Lysander declares his passion for her. The two youngsters are now at total cross-purposes with their earlier statements as well as with each other.

Helena, at first uncomprehending, gradually understands what Lysander means, and becomes more and more angry, interpreting his protestations of love as mockery. Instead of being grateful for his attentions, as he hopes, she scolds him fiercely, repeating her words to emphasise her fury and calling him 'young man' to show her disdain, before stalking off stage with all the dignity that, in her anger and self-pity, she can muster. Lysander pauses a moment to address the sleeping Hermia, so that we can see how hostile to her he has become, before going in pursuit of his futile love.

There is a strong change of tone when Hermia awakens. The much more varied rhythm of her speech makes it sound like an authentic utterance of feeling, in contrast to the neatly end-stopped couplets of the previous two speakers. The way she repeats Lysander's name shows her reaching out for companionship and protection in the darkness of the wood. After his desertion of her, it is only appropriate that Lysander should have appeared in her nightmare, smiling at her distress, although she cannot yet know this, unless, while sleeping, she subconsciously heard his rejection.

The serpent is a powerful **symbol** of danger, not only crystallising the vulnerability to wild animals Hermia feels when alone in the wood, but recalling the serpent in Genesis who tempted Eve to betray Adam. In fact, the serpent is a symbol of malice throughout the play. The fairies begin the lullaby for their queen by warning off 'spotted snakes with double tongue' (II.2.9) and in his epilogue Robin implores the audience not to respond to the play with 'the serpent's tongue' (V.1.423).

The short questions and exclamations which make up most of the second half of Hermia's speech are in effect alarmed cries which she utters as she rises and fearfully explores the stage. While we may be confident that everything will come right at the end of the play, her exit still leaves us in considerable suspense. What will she find? Will Helena still be rejecting Lysander? Will Lysander and Demetrius have come to blows? Shakespeare does not answer any of these questions immediately, but leaves them at the backs of our minds, instead taking us to another part of the wood where the craftsmen are just beginning their rehearsals.

TEXT 2   (III.1.1–65)

Enter the clowns: BOTTOM, QUINCE, SNOUT, STARVELING, FLUTE, *and* SNUG

BOTTOM: Are we all met?

QUINCE: Pat, pat; and here's a marvellous convenient place
for our rehearsal. This green plot shall be our stage, this
hawthorn brake our tiring-house, and we will do it in
action as we will do it before the Duke.

BOTTOM: Peter Quince!

QUINCE: What sayest thou, Bully Bottom?

BOTTOM: There are things in this comedy of Pyramus and
Thisbe that will never please. First, Pyramus must draw
a sword to kill himself, which the ladies cannot abide.
How answer you that?

SNOUT: By 'r lakin, a parlous fear!

STARVELING: I believe we must leave the killing out,
when all is done.

BOTTOM: Not a whit. I have a device to make all well. Write me a prologue, and let the prologue seem to say we will do no harm with our swords, and that Pyramus is not killed indeed; and for the more better assurance, tell them that I, Pyramus, am not Pyramus, but Bottom the weaver. This will put them out of fear.

QUINCE: Well, we will have such a prologue; and it shall be written in eight and six.

BOTTOM: No, make it two more: let it be written in eight and eight.

SNOUT: Will not the ladies be afeard of the lion?

STARVELING: I fear it, I promise you.

BOTTOM: Masters, you ought to consider with yourself, to bring in – God shield us – a lion among ladies is a most dreadful thing; for there is not a more fearful wildfowl than your lion living; and we ought to look to't.

SNOUT: Therefore another prologue must tell he is not a lion.

BOTTOM: Nay, you must name his name, and half his face must be seen through the lion's neck, and he himself must speak through, saying thus, or to the same defect: 'Ladies', or 'Fair ladies – I would wish you', or 'I would request you', or 'I would entreat you – not to fear, not to tremble. My life for yours: if you think I come hither as a lion, it were pity of my life. No. I am no such thing. I am a man, as other men are' – and there indeed let him name his name, and tell them plainly he is Snug the joiner.

QUINCE: Well, it shall be so. But there is two hard things: that is, to bring the moonlight into a chamber – for, you know, Pyramus and Thisbe meet by moonlight.

SNUG: Doth the moon shine that night we play our play?

BOTTOM: A calendar, a calendar! Look in the almanac – find out moonshine, find out moonshine!

QUINCE: Yes, it doth shine that night.

BOTTOM: Why, then, may you leave a casement of the
Great Chamber window – where we play – open, and
the moon may shine in at the casement.

QUINCE: Ay; or else one must come in with a bush of
thorns and a lantern, and say he comes to disfigure or to
present the person of Moonshine. Then there is another
thing. We must have a wall in the Great Chamber; for
Pyramus and Thisbe, says the story, did talk through the
chink of a wall.

SNOUT: You can never bring in a wall. What say you,
Bottom?

BOTTOM: Some man or other must present Wall; and let
him have some plaster, or some loam, or some roughcast
about him to signify Wall; and let him hold his fingers
thus, and through that cranny shall Pyramus and Thisbe whisper.

This is our second view of the craftsmen. Previously we have seen
them casting and discussing the staging of their play. Now they meet
in the wood to begin their rehearsal, although it soon becomes clear that
there are further technical problems to be resolved before this can take
place. The audience know, though the craftsmen do not, that the
wood also holds the fairies and the lovers, and the audience are therefore
not altogether surprised when the puck enters shortly after Bottom's
last speech and decides to enliven the proceedings. (In the First Folio, he
is actually indicated as entering twice, the first time at line 48, when
Bottom is shouting 'Find out moonshine!' It may be that in productions
of Shakespeare's time he did come in then and pass invisibly among the
craftsmen, or peer at them from the side, before coming forward to
address the audience at line 70.) We have already seen the fairies enter
the world of mortals when, at Oberon's bidding, Robin puts the magic
juice on Lysander's eyes. Throughout the opening of the present scene
we have some expectation that the craftsmen too will soon be affected by
the presence of the fairies.

    Bottom's opening question, 'Are we all met?' suggests he may be the
last to arrive; otherwise he would know who was there. It is typical of the

ebullience for which he is known as 'Bully Bottom' that he at once takes the initiative, but he is careful to work through the chairmanship of Peter Quince, who seems to be the originator of the project and who has the more methodical, detailed approach to it. It is Quince, for example, who carefully chooses the location for their rehearsal. The joke here is that the place is 'marvellous convenient' because the features are exactly what he says they are. The 'green plot' is an ideal stage because it is in fact the stage of the theatre, while the 'hawthorn brake' is the actual dressing room area.

Just as Bottom held up the proceedings in Act I Scene 2, so he now prevents the rehearsal beginning by stating an objection to the play which has occurred to him since their last meeting, that the drawing of a sword on stage will frighten the women in the audience. It has been suggested that this fear reflects violent unrest among artisans during the 1590s, which would have made the upper classes especially sensitive to a working man drawing a sword in their presence, but there is no evidence in the play that anyone finds this particular set of workers alarming. Rather the opposite. The craftsmen are looked down upon and laughed at by aristocrats and fairies alike.

The craftsmen's fear that the Athenian nobles will mistake Bottom and Snug for a valiant hero and a wild lion is funny precisely because they place such great faith in their own acting abilities and so little importance on the willing participation of the audience in the theatrical illusion. The nobles can believe that Bottom is the valiant Pyramus only in the same way that we can believe the stage to be a 'green plot'. Plainly anyone who goes to the theatre knows that what they are about to witness is art, not 'life'. It is true that they might at times become so caught up in what they see that their emotional reactions become similar to those of everyday reality, but it requires considerable dramatic experience to bring this about – considerably more than Quince and company possess. The craftsmen's naïveté is so great, however, that Starveling even suggests leaving out the death of Pyramus altogether.

Bottom's more constructive solution to the problem is to equip the play with a prologue which will reassure the audience that their **tragedy** is only an imitation of life. He is so enthusiastic that he wants the speech written in 'eight and eight', not a mere 'eight and six', not realising that the figures represent no more than the number of syllables per line.

Naturally, Bottom assumes that he will play the part of the prologue, so that his suggestion has the secondary benefit of giving him another role in the play. In the event, although Quince agrees to the suggestion, he manages to reallocate the part to himself before the performance.

A second objection comes from Snout, that the presence of a lion on stage may cause the female members of the audience just as much alarm as a sword. Bottom is quick to take up the point and elaborate it, showing again that he is the most confident public speaker among the craftsmen, and indeed the most grandiloquent, fussing over the exact form of address Snug should use when he speaks to the audience to explain he is not a lion. As usual, much of the humour in this scene comes from pretentious misuse of language. The lion is a fierce wild beast, not a 'fearful ... wildfowl', and Snug should be speaking to the same effect, not 'the same defect', although the latter may well be an unintentionally accurate description of his timid delivery.

Having accepted this second revision of the script, Quince has further theatrical problems to raise, although he seems to do so with a solution ready to hand which will impress the others. The first problem is 'to bring the moonlight into a chamber'. His fellow craftsmen, as he perhaps hoped they would, opt for the most obvious solution: opening the window so the moonlight can shine in, provided the moon shines on the wedding night. The craftsmen speak of looking up the date in an almanac – a book of dates, listing significant occasions such as anniversaries and astronomical events – but Quince's confident announcement that 'it doth shine that night' need not involve him consulting a book. He may have looked up the date earlier. In any case, he has a more dramatically satisfying solution that the simple opening of a window. One of the actors can act the part of Moonshine. His choice of the word 'disfigure' here is again comically appropriate, as Starveling, equipped with the traditional props of a lantern, a thorn bush and a dog, gives a very poor impression of magical, transforming light. In contrast, Shakespeare's many references to the moon and moonlight subtly create a night-time world where anything may prove possible.

Quince's second problem, how to bring a wall on stage, is dealt with in the same manner. An actor will play the wall. This time Bottom is first to propose the solution (though we may suspect that he snatches the words from Quince's mouth before the latter can say them) and, with his love of theatrical detail, he rejoices in envisaging the appropriate costume. Again, we may note how, in comparison, Shakespeare can create a palace and a wood on stage simply by the suggestive power of his language, and can create patterns of opposition and marrying together throughout the play without the need of physical walls to make the point clear.

TEXT 3   (III.2.346–412)

OBERON *and* PUCK *come forward*

OBERON:

This is thy negligence. Still thou mistakest,
Or else committest thy knaveries wilfully.

PUCK:

Believe me, King of shadows, I mistook.
Did you not tell me I should know the man
By the Athenian garments he had on?
And so far blameless proves my enterprise
That I have 'nointed an Athenian's eyes.
And so far am I glad it so did sort,
As this their jangling I esteem a sport.

OBERON:

Thou seest these lovers seek a place to fight.
Hie therefore, Robin, overcast the night.
The starry welkin cover thou anon
With drooping fog as black as Acheron,
And lead these testy rivals so astray
As one come not within another's way.
Like to Lysander sometimes frame thy tongue,
Then stir Demetrius up with bitter wrong,
And sometimes rail thou like Demetrius;
And from each other look thou lead them thus
Till o'er their brows death-counterfeiting sleep
With leaden legs and batty wings doth creep.
Then crush this herb into Lysander's eye –
Whose liquor hath this virtuous property,

To take from thence all error with his might,
And make his eyeballs roll with wonted sight.
When they next wake, all this derision
Shall seem a dream and fruitless vision,
And back to Athens shall the lovers wend
With league whose date till death shall never end.
Whiles I in this affair do thee employ
I'll to my Queen and beg her Indian boy,
And then I will her charmèd eye release
From monster's view, and all things shall be peace.

PUCK:

My fairy lord, this must be done with haste,
For night's swift dragons cut the clouds full fast,
And yonder shines Aurora's harbinger,
At whose approach ghosts wandering here and there
Troop home to churchyards. Damnèd spirits all
That in crossways and floods have burial
Already to their wormy beds are gone.
For fear lest day should look their shames upon
They wilfully themselves exile from light,
And must for aye consort with black-browed night.

OBERON:

But we are spirits of another sort.
I with the morning's love have oft made sport,
And like a forester the groves may tread
Even till the eastern gate all fiery red
Opening on Neptune with fair blessèd beams
Turns into yellow gold his salt green streams.
But notwithstanding, haste, make no delay;
We may effect this business yet ere day.   *Exit*

PUCK:

Up and down, up and down,
I will lead them up and down.
I am feared in field and town.
Goblin, lead them up and down.
Here comes one.

Enter LYSANDER

LYSANDER:
Where art thou, proud Demetrius? Speak thou now.

PUCK (*in Demetrius's voice*):
Here, villain, drawn and ready! Where art thou?

LYSANDER:
I will be with thee straight.

PUCK (*in Demetrius's voice*): Follow me then
To plainer ground.   *Exit* LYSANDER

Enter DEMETRIUS

DEMETRIUS: Lysander, speak again.
Thou runaway, thou coward – art thou fled?
Speak. In some bush? Where dost thou hide thy head?

PUCK (*in Lysander's voice*):
Thou coward, art thou bragging to the stars,
Telling the bushes that thou lookest for wars,
And wilt not come? Come, recreant. Come, thou child,
I'll whip thee with a rod. He is defiled
That draws a sword on thee.

DEMETRIUS: Yea, art thou there?

PUCK (*in Lysander's voice*):
Follow my voice. We'll try no manhood here.

Exeunt PUCK *and* DEMETRIUS

The four lovers have by this section of the play reached the point of their greatest confusion. Both Lysander and Demetrius have had the magic juice put on their eyes and, as a result, alike have fallen for Helena and rejected Hermia. Under their spell, they regard this as entirely natural behaviour, but the two women are baffled by the unexpected development. Helena assumes that the men's love is only a pretence and that they are really making fun of her, concluding that, in the light of their past devotion, this must be because Hermia has told them to do so. Hermia meanwhile, after her initial disbelief at Lysander's alteration, has become convinced that Helena must have seduced him away from her and in reaction she tries to physically assault her rival. Violence also springs up between the men. Intending to fight over who shall have Helena, Lysander and Demetrius stride off to find a suitable place to hold a duel. Helena then runs fearfully from Hermia, who pursues her, though by this time more in bafflement than in anger.

After the rhyming couplets of Helena and Hermia, Oberon's first two unrhyming lines create a minor irregularity in the sound of the verse which signals the return to dramatic prominence of himself and the puck. It is possible that they have been off-stage during the argument between the lovers so that they will not distract the audience from the action, but Oberon's earlier command to Robin ('Stand aside') is a vague one and it is more likely that they have merely been positioned unobtrusively to one side. Oberon and Robin have been spectators of the quarrel and, as observers of them in turn, the audience are interested to find out their response to it, especially since they seem likely to intervene in the next stage of the mortals' dispute. Just as we have been entertained by the chaotic relationships of the lovers, so we are entertained now by the confusion of the fairy king, whose efforts to help the humans have ironically made the situation even worse than it was before.

In the present scene Oberon and Robin are something of a double act, with Oberon taking the part of the 'straight man', scolding the puck for his bungled mission. In some productions, this relationship may be shown physically, with Oberon taking hold of the puck or pushing him round the stage. The incorrigible Robin, though defensive at first and keen to make his excuses, rapidly shifts the blame back onto Oberon (whose orders he has, after all, followed to the letter) and is unrepentant about enjoying the outcome of his error as much as we in the audience have done. He addresses Oberon here as 'King of shadows' because the fairies are mysterious creatures, not fully perceived and understood by mortals, and are active in the concealing night, not the broad light of day. However, the phrase also anticipates Theseus's description of actors as shadows (V.1.208), and eventually Robin will bring the two meanings together in his epilogue with the phrase 'we shadows' (see Themes on Theatre).

Oberon's long speech beginning, 'Thou seest these lovers,' is a highly reassuring one, which takes the suspense out of the story to a remarkable extent. He explains how Robin can prevent violence between Lysander and Demetrius, and how the end result will be the lovers' return to Athens in an amity which 'till death shall never end'. It is unusual to be told so far from the conclusion of a play, let alone so authoritatively, that characters will live happily ever after. Oberon even seems sure that Titania will let him have the little boy who was the object of their quarrel, and in predicting that for the lovers 'all this derision / Shall seem a dream' he even anticipates the epilogue, where Robin says much the same about the play as a whole. Clearly Shakespeare no longer wishes us to be in suspense about the outcome of the lovers' conflicts. Having been brought to the point of maximum tension, these will now be resolved, and new sources of dramatic interest be brought in to replace them, on which we can focus without distraction, particularly the staging of 'Pyramus and Thisbe'.

The decisiveness and confidence with which Oberon speaks is typical of his supernatural authority, and indeed the comparatively heavy **end-stopping** of these lines gives them something of the chanted rhythm of a spell. Some of the **imagery** has a sinister quality which adds to the seriousness of tone: 'black as Acheron … death-counterfeiting sleep / With leaden legs and batty wings'. This tone is picked up and amplified in the puck's reply with its gruesome references to 'ghosts' and their 'wormy beds'. However, this proves to be an opportunity for Oberon to emphasise that the fairies are 'spirits of another sort'. If they are not at home in the full glare of daylight, they are at least able to continue their activities for the duration of dawn, unlike evil spirits who cannot bear any sunlight. A Christian who believed in the existence of fairies would be hard pressed to account for their origin without explaining them as disguised demons. Where could they come from but Hell? Shakespeare is anxious that we see the fairies positively, as **personifications** of the forces of nature, and appropriately Oberon himself now employs personification. Robin has already spoken of the dawn as the goddess Aurora. Oberon goes on to claim that he has exercised his masculine charms on her, and speaks of the sea in the form of the sea god Neptune. Does the puck sing or speak the next lines?:

> Up and down, up and down,
> I will lead them up and down. (III.2.396–7)

As on several other occasions when Robin or the fairies shift their speech into short rhyming lines, it would be possible to sing them, either with or without musical accompaniment. They certainly mark a transition from conversation to enchantment, and we can now sit back and enjoy the trickery through which Robin draws the two young men apart.

The type of stage on which actors performed in the Elizabethan era made little use of scenery (see Shakespeare's Theatre). It was possible, therefore, to change locations, or split the stage between several locations, by the use of language alone. When Lysander enters, we do not have to assume that he is wandering back into the place he had left earlier. Robin can move towards him, indicating that he is moving to a different part of the wood to find him. Similarly, when Lysander leaves and Demetrius appears, Robin can race over to him. As the puck dances around the two men, calling out to each in turn, their acting and the imagination of the audience furnish the bare stage with the bushes of which they speak. In our mind's eye we see Robin hiding behind branches and the two rivals clambering through an intricate forest. In film and television productions, the puck is able to perfectly imitate the voices of his two victims by lip-synching to tapes of them. On stage it is easy enough for him to approximate their voices and the other two actors to respond accordingly. Whatever our reservations about the tricks Robin plays on Titania and Bottom, we enjoy seeing the two young men who have rejected Hermia (and, in the case of Demetrius, Helena) thoroughly tormented and misled.

PART FIVE

Background

William shakespeare's life

There are no personal records of Shakespeare's life. Official documents and occasional references to him by contemporary dramatists enable us to draw the main outline of his public life, but his private life remains hidden. Although not at all unusual for a writer of his time, this lack of first-hand evidence has tempted many to read his plays as personal records and to look to them for clues to his character and convictions. The results are unconvincing, partly because Renaissance art was not subjective or designed primarily to express its creator's personality, and partly because the drama of any period is very difficult to read biographically. Except when plays are written by committed dramatists to promote social or political causes (as by Shaw or Brecht), it is all but impossible to decide who amongst the variety of fictional characters in a drama represents the dramatist, or which of the various and often conflicting points of view expressed is authorial.

What we do know can be quickly summarised. Shakespeare was born into a well-to-do family in the market town of Stratford-upon-Avon in Warwickshire, where he was baptised, in Holy Trinity Church, on 26 April 1564. His father, John Shakespeare, was a prosperous glover and leather merchant who became a person of some importance in the town: in 1565 he was elected an alderman of the town, and in 1568 he became high bailiff (or mayor) of Stratford. In 1557 he had married Mary Arden. Their third child (of eight) and eldest son, William, learned to read and write at the primary (or 'petty') school in Stratford and then, it seems probable, attended the local grammar school, where he would have studied Latin, history, logic and rhetoric. In November 1582 William, then aged eighteen, married Anne Hathaway, who was twenty-six years old. They had a daughter, Susanna, in May 1583, and twins, Hamnet and Judith, in 1585.

Shakespeare next appears in the historical record in 1592 when he is mentioned as a London actor and playwright in a pamphlet by the dramatist Robert Greene. These 'lost years' 1585–92 have been the subject of much speculation, but how they were occupied remains as much a mystery as when Shakespeare left Stratford, and why. In his pamphlet, *Greene's Groatsworth of Wit*, Greene expresses to his fellow dramatists his outrage that the 'upstart crow' Shakespeare has the impudence to believe he 'is as well able to bombast out a blank verse as the best of you'. To have aroused this hostility from a rival, Shakespeare must, by 1592, have been long enough in London to have made a name for himself as a playwright. We may conjecture that he had left Stratford in 1586 or 1587.

During the next twenty years, Shakespeare continued to live in London, regularly visiting his wife and family in Stratford. He continued to act, but his chief fame was as a dramatist. From 1594 he wrote exclusively for the Lord Chamberlain's Men, which rapidly became the leading dramatic company and from 1603 enjoyed the patronage of James I as the King's Men. His plays were extremely popular and he became a shareholder in his theatre company. He was able to buy lands around Stratford and a large house in the town, to which he retired about 1611. He died there on 23 April 1616 and was buried in Holy Trinity Church on 25 April.

SHAKESPEARE'S DRAMATIC CAREER

Between the late 1580s and 1613 Shakespeare wrote thirty-seven plays, and contributed to some by other dramatists. This was by no means an exceptional number for a professional playwright of the times. The exact date of the composition of individual plays is a matter of debate – for only a few plays is the date of their first performance known – but the broad outlines of Shakespeare's dramatic career have been established. He began in the late 1580s and early 1590s by rewriting earlier plays and working with plotlines inspired by the Classics. He concentrated on **comedies** (such as *The Comedy of Errors*, 1590–4, which derived from the Latin playwright Plautus) and plays dealing with English history (such as the three parts of *Henry VI*, 1589–92), though he also tried his hand at bloodthirsty revenge **tragedy** (*Titus Andronicus*, 1592–3, indebted to both Ovid and Seneca). During the 1590s Shakespeare developed his expertise in these kinds of play to write comic masterpieces such as *A Midsummer Night's Dream* (1594–5) and *As You*

Like It (1599–1600) and history plays such as *Henry IV* (1596–8) and *Henry V* (1598–9).

As the new century begins a new note is detectable. Plays such as *Troilus and Cressida* (1601–2) and *Measure for Measure* (1603–4), poised between comedy and tragedy, evoke complex responses. Because of their generic uncertainty and ambivalent tone such works are sometimes referred to as 'problem plays', but it is tragedy which comes to dominate the extraordinary sequence of masterpieces: *Hamlet* (1600–1), *Othello* (1602–4), *King Lear* (1605–6), *Macbeth* (1605–6) and *Antony and Cleopatra* (1606).

In the last years of his dramatic career, Shakespeare wrote a group of plays of a quite different kind. These 'romances', as they are often called, are in many ways the most remarkable of all his plays. The group comprises *Pericles* (1608), *Cymbeline* (1609–11), *The Winter's Tale* (1610–11) and *The Tempest* (1610–11). These plays (particularly *Cymbeline*) reprise many of the situations and themes of the earlier dramas but in fantastical and exotic dramatic designs which, set in distant lands, covering large tracts of time and involving music, mime, dance and tableaux, have something of the qualities of masques and pageants. The situations which in the tragedies had led to disaster are here resolved: the great theme is restoration and reconciliation. Where in the tragedies Ophelia, Desdemona and Cordelia died, the daughters of these plays – Marina, Imogen, Perdita, Miranda – survive and are reunited with their parents and lovers.

THE TEXTS OF SHAKESPEARE'S PLAYS

Nineteen of Shakespeare's plays were printed during his lifetime in what are called 'quartos' (books, each containing one play, and made up of sheets of paper each folded twice to make four leaves). Shakespeare, however, did not supervise their publication. This was not unusual. When a playwright had sold a play to a dramatic company he sold his rights in it: copyright belonged to whoever had possession of an actual copy of the text, and so consequently authors had no control over what happened to their work. Anyone who could get hold of the text of a play might publish it if they wished. Hence, what found its way into print might be the author's copy, but it might be an actor's copy or prompt copy, perhaps cut or altered for performance; sometimes, actors (or even members of the audience) might publish what they could remember of the text. Printers, working without the benefit of the author's oversight, introduced their own errors, through misreading the manuscript for example, and by 'correcting' what seemed to them not to make sense.

In 1623 John Heminges and Henry Condell, two actors in Shakespeare's company, collected together texts of thirty-six of Shakespeare's plays (*Pericles* was omitted) and published them in a large folio (a book in which each sheet of paper is folded once in half, to give two leaves). This, the First Folio, was followed by later editions in 1632, 1663 and 1685. Despite its appearance of authority, however, the texts in the First Folio still present many difficulties, for there are printing errors and confused passages in the plays, and its texts often differ significantly from those of the earlier quartos, when these exist.

Shakespeare's texts have, then, been through a number of intermediaries. We do not have his authority for any one of his plays, and hence we cannot know exactly what it was that he wrote. Bibliographers, textual critics and editors have spent a great deal of effort on endeavouring to get behind the errors, uncertainties and contradictions in the available texts to recover the plays as Shakespeare originally wrote them. What we read is the result of these efforts. Modern texts are what editors have constructed from the available evidence: they correspond to no sixteenth- or seventeenth-century editions, and to no early performance of a Shakespeare play. Furthermore, these composite texts differ from each other, for different editors read the early texts differently and come to different conclusions. A Shakespeare text is an unstable and a contrived thing.

Often, of course, its judgements embody, if not the personal prejudices of the editor, then the cultural preferences of the time in which he or she was working. Growing awareness of this has led recent scholars to distrust the whole editorial enterprise and to repudiate the attempt to construct a 'perfect' text. Stanley Wells and Gary Taylor, the editors of the Oxford edition of *The Complete Works* (1986), point out that almost certainly the texts of Shakespeare's plays were altered in performance, and from one performance to another, so that there may never have been a single version. They note, too, that Shakespeare probably revised and rewrote some plays. They do not claim to print a definitive text of any play, but prefer what seems to them the 'more theatrical' version, and when there is a great difference between available versions, as with *King Lear*, they print two texts.

SHAKESPEARE & THE ENGLISH RENAISSANCE

Shakespeare arrived in London at the very time that the Elizabethan period was poised to become the 'golden age' of English literature. Although Elizabeth reigned as Queen from 1558 to 1603, the term 'Elizabethan' is used very loosely in a literary sense to refer to the period 1580 to 1625, when the great works of the age were produced. (Sometimes the later part of this period is distinguished as 'Jacobean', from the Latin form of the name of the king who succeeded Elizabeth, James I of England and VI of Scotland, who reigned from 1603 to 1625.) The poet Edmund Spenser heralded this new age with his **pastoral** poem *The Shepheardes Calender* (1579) and in his essay *An Apologie for Poetrie* (written about 1580, although not published until 1595) his friend Sir Philip Sidney championed the imaginative power of the 'speaking picture of poesy', famously declaring that 'Nature never set forth the earth in so rich a tapestry as divers poets have done ... Her world is brazen, the poet's only deliver a golden'.

Spenser and Sidney were part of that rejuvenating movement in European culture which since the nineteenth century has been known by the term *Renaissance*. Meaning literally *rebirth* it denotes a revival and redirection of artistic and intellectual endeavour which began in Italy in the fourteenth century in the poetry of Petrarch. It spread gradually northwards across Europe, and is first detectable in England in the early sixteenth century in the writings of the scholar and statesman Sir Thomas More and in the poetry of Sir Thomas Wyatt and Henry Howard, Earl of Surrey. Its keynote was a curiosity in thought which challenged old assumptions and traditions. To the innovative spirit of the Renaissance, the preceding ages appeared dully unoriginal and conformist.

That spirit was fuelled by the rediscovery of many classical texts and the culture of Greece and Rome. This fostered a confidence in human reason and in human potential which, in every sphere, challenged old convictions. The discovery of America and its peoples (Columbus had sailed in 1492) demonstrated that the world was a larger and stranger place than had been thought. The cosmological speculation of Copernicus (later confirmed by Galileo) that the sun, not the earth was the centre of our planetary system challenged the centuries-old belief that the earth and human beings were at the centre of the cosmos. The pragmatic political philosophy of Machiavelli seemed to cut politics free from its traditional link with morality by permitting to statesmen any means which secured the desired end. And the religious movements we know collectively as the Reformation broke with the Church of Rome and set the individual conscience, not ecclesiastical authority, at the centre of the religious life. Nothing, it seemed, was beyond questioning, nothing impossible.

Shakespeare's drama is innovative and challenging in exactly the way of the Renaissance. It questions the beliefs, assumptions and politics upon which Elizabethan society was founded. And although the plays always conclude in a restoration of order and stability, many critics are inclined to argue that their imaginative energy goes into subverting, rather than reinforcing, traditional values. Convention, audience expectation and censorship all required the status quo to be endorsed by the **plots**' conclusions, but the dramas find ways to allow alternative sentiments to be expressed. Frequently, figures of authority are undercut by some comic or parodic figure. Despairing, critical, dissident, disillusioned, unbalanced, rebellious, mocking voices are repeatedly to be heard in the plays, rejecting, resenting, defying the established order. They belong always to marginal, socially unacceptable figures, 'licensed', as it were, by their situations to say what would be unacceptable from socially privileged or responsible citizens. The question is: are such characters given these views to discredit them, or were they the only ones through whom a voice could be given to radical and dissident ideas? Is Shakespeare a conservative or a revolutionary?

Renaissance culture was intensely nationalistic. With the break-up of the internationalism of the Middle Ages the evolving nation states which still mark the map of Europe began for the first time to acquire distinctive cultural identities. There was intense rivalry among them as they sought to achieve in their own vernacular languages a culture which could equal that of Greece and Rome. Spenser's great allegorical epic poem *The Faerie Queene*, which began to appear from 1590, celebrated

Elizabeth and was intended to outdo the poetic achievements of France and Italy and to stand beside works of Virgil and Homer. Shakespeare is equally preoccupied with national identity. His history plays tell an epic story which examines how modern England came into being through the conflicts of the fifteenth-century Wars of the Roses which brought the Tudors to the throne. He is fascinated, too, by the related subject of politics and the exercise of power. With the collapse of medieval feudalism and the authority of local barons, the royal court in the Renaissance came to assume a new status as the centre of power and patronage. It was here that the destiny of a country was shaped. Courts, and how to succeed in them, consequently fascinated the Renaissance; and they fascinated Shakespeare and his audience.

But the dramatic gaze is not merely admiring; through a variety of devices, a critical perspective is brought to bear. The court may be paralleled by a very different world, revealing uncomfortable similarities (for example, Henry's court and the Boar's Head tavern, ruled over by Falstaff in *Henry IV*). Its hypocrisy may be bitterly denounced (for example, in the diatribes of the mad Lear) and its self-seeking ambition represented disturbingly in the figure of a Machiavellian villain (such as Edmund in *Lear*) or a malcontent (such as Iago in *Othello*). Shakespeare is fond of displacing the court to another context, the better to examine its assumptions and pretensions and to offer alternatives to the courtly life (for example, in the **pastoral** setting of the forest of Arden in *As You Like It* or Prospero's island in *The Tempest*). Courtiers are frequently figures of fun whose unmanly sophistication ('neat and trimly dressed, / Fresh as a bridegroom ... perfumed like a milliner', says Hotspur of such a man in *1 Henry IV*, I.3.33–6) is contrasted with plain-speaking integrity: Oswald is set against Kent in *King Lear*.

(When thinking of these matters, we should remember that stage plays were subject to censorship, and any criticism had therefore to be muted or oblique: direct criticism of the monarch or contemporary English court would not be tolerated. This has something to do with why Shakespeare's plays are always set either in the past, or abroad.)

The nationalism of the English Renaissance was reinforced by Protestantism. Henry VIII had broken with Rome in the 1530s and in Shakespeare's time there was an independent Protestant state church. Because the Pope in Rome had excommunicated Queen Elizabeth as a heretic and relieved the English of their allegiance to the Crown, there was deep suspicion of Roman Catholics as potential traitors. This was enforced by the attempted invasion of the Spanish Armada in 1588. This was a religiously inspired crusade to overthrow Elizabeth and restore England to Roman Catholic allegiance. Roman Catholicism was hence easily identified with hostility to England. Its association with disloyalty and treachery was enforced by the Gunpowder Plot of 1605, a Roman Catholic attempt to destroy the government of England.

Shakespeare's plays are remarkably free from direct religious sentiment, but their emphases are Protestant. Young women, for example, are destined for marriage, not for nunneries (precisely the fate with which Hermia is threatened in the opening scene of *A Midsummer Night's Dream*); friars are dubious characters, full of schemes and deceptions, if with benign intentions, as in *Much Ado About Nothing* or *Romeo and Juliet*. (We should add, though, that Puritans, extreme Protestants, are even less kindly treated: for example, Malvolio in *Twelfth Night*.)

The central figures of the plays are frequently individuals beset by temptation, by the lure of evil – Angelo in *Measure for Measure*, Othello, Lear, Macbeth – and not only in tragedies: Falstaff is described as 'that old white-bearded Satan' (*1 Henry IV*, II.4.454). We follow their inner struggles. Shakespeare's heroes have the preoccupation with self and the introspective tendencies encouraged by Protestantism: his tragic heroes are haunted by their consciences, seeking their true selves, agonising over what course of action to take as they follow what can often be understood as a kind of spiritual progress towards heaven or hell.

SHAKESPEARE'S THEATRE

The theatre for which the plays were written was one of the most remarkable innovations of the Renaissance. There had been no theatres or acting companies during the medieval period. Performed on carts and in open spaces at Christian festivals, plays had been almost exclusively religious. Such professional actors as there were wandered the country putting on a variety of entertainments in the yards of inns, on makeshift stages in market squares, or anywhere else suitable. They did not perform

THE GLOBE THEATRE,

On the   Bankside.

As it appeared in the reign of King James I.

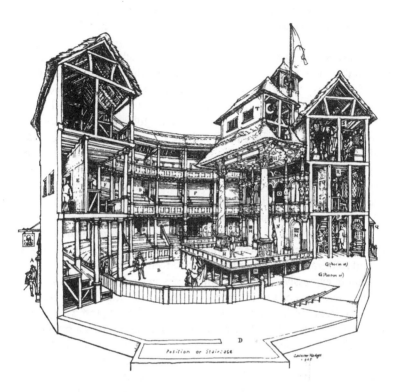

A CONJECTURAL RECONSTRUCTION OF THE INTERIOR OF THE GLOBE PLAYHOUSE

AA   Main entrance
B   The Yard
CC   Entrances to lowest galleries
D   Entrance to staircase and upper galleries
E   Corridor serving the different sections of the middle gallery
F   Middle gallery ('Twopenny Rooms')
G   'Gentlemen's Rooms or Lords Rooms'
H   The stage
J   The hanging being put up round the stage
K   The 'Hell' under the stage
L   The stage trap, leading down to the Hell
MM   Stage doors

N   Curtained 'place behind the stage'
O   Gallery above the stage, used as required sometimes by musicians, sometimes by spectators, and often as part of the play
P   Back-stage area (the tiring-house)
Q   Tiring-house door
R   Dressing-rooms
S   Wardrobe and storage
T   The hut housing the machine for lowering enthroned gods, etc., to the stage
U   The 'Heavens'
W   Hoisting the playhouse flag

full-length plays, but mimes, juggling and comedy acts. Such actors were regarded by officialdom and polite society as little better than vagabonds and layabouts.

Just before Shakespeare went to London all this began to change. A number of young men who had been to the universities of Oxford and Cambridge came to London in the 1580s and began to write plays which made use of what they had learned about the Classical Drama of ancient Greece and Rome. Plays such as John Lyly's *Alexander and Campaspe* (1584), Christopher Marlowe's *Tamburlaine the Great* (about 1587) and Thomas Kyd's *The Spanish Tragedy* (1588–9) were unlike anything that had been written in English before. They were full-length plays on secular subjects, taking their **plots** from history and legend, adopting many of the devices of Classical Drama, and offering a range of **characterisation** and situation hitherto unattempted in English drama. With the exception of Lyly's **prose** dramas, they were in the unrhymed **iambic pentameters (blank verse)** which the Earl of Surrey had introduced into English earlier in the sixteenth century. This was a freer and more expressive medium than the rhymed **verse** of medieval drama. It was the drama of these 'university wits' which Shakespeare challenged when he came to London. Greene was one of them, and we have heard how little he liked this Shakespeare setting himself up as a dramatist.

The most significant change of all, however, was that these dramatists wrote for the professional theatre. In 1576 James Burbage built the first permanent theatre in England, in Shoreditch, just beyond London's northern boundary. It was called simply 'The Theatre'. Others soon followed. Thus, when Shakespeare came to London, there was a flourishing drama, theatres and companies of actors waiting for him, such as there had never been before in England. His company performed at James Burbage's Theatre until 1596, and used the Swan and Curtain until they moved into their own new theatre, the Globe, in 1599. It was burned down in 1613 when a cannon was fired during a performance of Shakespeare's *Henry VIII*.

With the completion in 1996 of Sam Wanamaker's project to construct in London a replica of The Globe, and with productions now running there, a version of Shakespeare's theatre can be experienced at first-hand. It is very different to the usual modern experience of drama. The form of the Elizabethan theatre derived from the inn yards and animal baiting rings in which actors had been accustomed to perform in the past. They were circular wooden buildings with a paved courtyard in the middle open to the sky. A rectangular stage jutted out into the middle of this yard. Some of the audience stood in the yard (or 'pit') to watch the play. They were thus on three sides of the stage, close up to it and on a level with it. These 'groundlings' paid only a penny to get in, but for wealthier spectators there were seats in three covered tiers or galleries between the inner and outer walls of the building, extending round most of the auditorium and overlooking the pit and the stage. Such a theatre could hold about 3,000 spectators. The yards were about 80ft in diameter and the rectangular stage approximately 40ft by 30ft and 5ft 6in high. Shakespeare aptly called such a theatre a 'wooden O' in the Prologue to *Henry V* (line 13).

The stage itself was partially covered by a roof or canopy which projected from the wall at the rear of the stage and was supported by two posts at the front. This protected the stage and performers from inclement weather, and to it were secured winches and other machinery for stage effects. On either side at the back of the stage was a door. These led into the dressing room (or 'tiring house') and it was by means of these doors that actors entered and left the stage. Between these doors was a small recess or alcove which was curtained off. Such a 'discovery place' served, for example, for Titania's bower when in Act II Scene 2 and Act III Scene 1 of *A Midsummer Night's Dream* she lies sleeping on her flowery bed. Above the discovery place was a balcony, used for the famous balcony scenes of *Romeo and Juliet* (II.2 and III.5), or for the battlements of Richard's castle when he is confronted by Bolingbroke in *Richard II* (III.3). Actors (all parts in the Elizabethan theatre were taken by boys or men) had access to the area beneath the stage; from here, in the 'cellarage', would have come the voice of the ghost of Hamlet's father (*Hamlet*, II.1.150–82).

On these stages there was very little in the way of scenery or props – there was nowhere to store them (there were no wings in this theatre) nor any way to set them up (no tabs across the stage), and, anyway, productions had to be transportable for performance at court or at noble houses. The stage was bare, which is why characters often tell us where they are: there was nothing on the stage to indicate location. It is also why location is so rarely topographical, and much more often **symbolic**. It suggests a dramatic mood or situation, rather than a place: Lear's barren heath reflects his destitute state, as the storm his emotional turmoil.

None of the plays printed in Shakespeare's lifetime marks Act or scene divisions. These have been introduced by later editors, but they should not mislead us into supposing that there was any break in Elizabethan performances such as might happen today while the curtains are closed and the set is changed. The staging of Elizabethan plays was continuous, with the many short 'scenes' of which Shakespeare's plays are often constructed following one after another in quick succession. We have to think of a more fluid and much faster production than we are generally used to: in the prologues to *Romeo and Juliet* (line 12) and *Henry VIII* (line 13) Shakespeare speaks of only two hours as the playing time. It is because plays were staged continuously that exits and entrances are written in as part of the script: characters speak as they enter or leave the stage because otherwise there would be a silence while, in full view, they took up their positions. (This is also why dead bodies are carried off: they cannot get up and walk off.)

In 1608 Shakespeare's company, the King's Men, acquired the Blackfriars Theatre, a smaller, rectangular indoor theatre, holding about 700 people, with seats for all the members of the audience, facilities for elaborate stage effects and, because it was enclosed, artificial lighting. It has been suggested that the plays written for this 'private' theatre differed from those written for The Globe, since, as it cost more to go to a private theatre, the audience came from a higher social stratum and demanded the more elaborate and courtly entertainment which Shakespeare's romances provide. However, the King's Men continued to play in The Globe in the summer, using Blackfriars in the winter, and it is not certain that Shakespeare's last plays were written specifically for the Blackfriars Theatre, or first performed there.

READING SHAKESPEARE

Shakespeare's plays were written for this stage, but there is also a sense in which they were written *by* this stage. The material and physical circumstances of their production in such theatres had a profound effect upon the nature of Elizabethan plays. Unless we bear this in mind, we are likely to find them very strange, for we will read with expectations shaped by our own familiarity with modern fiction and modern drama. This is, by and large, realistic; it seeks to persuade us that what we are reading or watching is really happening. This is quite foreign to Shakespeare. If we try to read him like this, we shall find ourselves irritated by the improbabilities of his plot, confused by his chronology, puzzled by locations, frustrated by unanswered questions and dissatisfied by the motivation of the action. The absurd ease with which disguised persons pass through Shakespeare's plays is a case in point: why does no-one recognise people they know so well? There is a great deal of psychological accuracy in Shakespeare's plays, but we are far from any attempt at realism.

The reason is that in Shakespeare's theatre it was impossible to pretend that the audience was not watching a contrived performance. In a modern theatre, the audience is encouraged to forget itself as it becomes absorbed by the action on stage. The worlds of the spectators and of the actors are sharply distinguished by the lighting: in the dark auditorium the audience is passive, silent, anonymous, receptive and attentive; on the lighted stage the actors are active, vocal, demonstrative and dramatic. (The distinction is, of course, still more marked in the cinema.) There is no communication between the two worlds: for the audience to speak would be interruptive; for the actors to address the audience would be to break the illusion of the play. In the Elizabethan theatre, this distinction did not exist, and for two reasons: first, performances took place in the open air and in daylight which illuminated everyone equally; secondly, the spectators were all around the stage (and wealthier spectators actually on it), and were dressed no differently to the actors, who wore contemporary dress. (An exception to this would be supernatural characters, such as the fairies in *A Midsummer Night's Dream*, who would have worn costumes inspired by folklore.) In such a theatre, spectators would be as aware of each other as of the actors; they could not lose their identity in a corporate group, nor could they ever forget that they were spectators at a performance. There was no chance that they could believe 'this is really happening'.

This, then, was communal theatre, not only in the sense that it was going on in the middle of a crowd but in the sense that the crowd joined in. Elizabethan audiences had none of our deference: they did not keep quiet, or arrive on time, or remain for the whole performance. They joined in, interrupted, even getting on the stage. And plays were preceded and followed by jigs and clowning. It was all much more like our experience of a pantomime, and at a pantomime we are fully aware, and are meant to be aware, that we are watching games being played with reality. The conventions of pantomime revel in their own artificiality: the fishnet tights are to signal that the handsome prince is a woman, the Dame's monstrous false breasts signal that 'she' is a man.

Something very similar is the case with Elizabethan theatre: it utilised its very theatricality. Instead of trying to persuade spectators that they are not in a theatre watching a performance, Elizabethan plays acknowledge the presence of the audience. It is addressed not only by prologues, epilogues and choruses, but in **soliloquies**. There is no realistic reason why characters should suddenly explain themselves to empty rooms, but, of course, it is not an empty room. The actor is surrounded by people. Soliloquies are not addressed to the world of the play: they are for the audience's benefit. And that audience's complicity is assumed: when a character like Oberon declares himself to be invisible, it is accepted that he is. Disguises are taken to be impenetrable, however improbable, and we are to accept impossibly contrived situations, such as barely hidden characters remaining undetected (indeed, on the Elizabethan stage there was nowhere at all they could hide).

These, then, are plays which are aware of themselves as dramas; in critical terminology, they are self-reflexive, commenting upon themselves as dramatic pieces and prompting the audience to think about the theatrical experience. They do this not only through their direct address to the audience but through their fondness for the play-within-a-play (which reminds the audience that the encompassing play is also a play) and their constant use of **images** from, and allusions to, the theatre. They are fascinated by role playing, by acting, appearance and reality. Things are rarely what they seem, either in **comedy** (for example, in *A Midsummer Night's Dream*) or **tragedy** (*Romeo and Juliet*). This offers one way to think about those disguises: they are thematic rather than realistic. Kent's disguise in *Lear* reveals his true, loyal self, while Edmund, who is not disguised, hides his true self. In *As You Like It*, Rosalind is more truly herself disguised as a man than when dressed as a woman.

The effect of all this is to confuse the distinction we would make between 'real life' and 'acting'. The case of Rosalind, for example, raises searching questions about gender roles, about how far it is 'natural' to be womanly or manly: how does the stage, on which a man can play a woman playing a man (and have a man fall in love with him/her), differ from life, in which we assume the roles we think appropriate to masculine and feminine behaviour? The same is true of political roles: when a Richard II or Lear is so aware of the regal part he is performing, of the trappings and rituals of kingship, their plays raise the uncomfortable possibility that the answer to the question, what constitutes a successful king, is simply: a good actor. Indeed, human life generally is repeatedly rendered through the imagery of the stage, from Macbeth's 'Life's but a walking shadow, a poor player / That struts and frets his hour upon the stage / And then is heard no more' (V.5.23–5) to Prospero's paralleling of human life to a performance which, like the globe (both world and theatre) will end (IV.I.146–58). When life is a fiction, like this play, or this play is a fiction like life, what is the difference? 'All the world's a stage ...' (*As You Like It*, II.7.139).

LITERARY BACKGROUND

Shakespeare's usual practice in creating a play was to explore the dramatic potential of an existing story. However, the three interlinking tales of *A Midsummer Night's Dream* (the lovers in the forest, the quarrel between Titania and Oberon, the staging of a play by inexperienced craftsmen) all seem to be his own invention. The only other dramas in the Shakespeare canon which are thought to be similarly original are *Love's Labour's Lost* and *The Tempest*. *The Tempest*, although written about fifteen years after *A Midsummer Night's Dream*, exhibits several telling similarities. Like Oberon, Prospero is a domineering but well-meaning authority figure who directs the events to a positive outcome, while the contrast between the earthy Bottom and the playful spirit Robin is developed to a greater extreme in Caliban and Ariel. Both plays conclude with the suggestion that life is like a theatrical performance or a dream.

If Shakespeare invented *A Midsummer Night's Dream*, he still took many of its ingredients from his reading. One major influence is Ovid's *Metamorphoses*, a book of verse which he knew in the original Latin and in English translation, having almost certainly studied it first at school.

Ovid recounts myths and legends, in each of which a supernatural transformation occurs which accounts for some phenomenon in the natural world. The story of Pyramus and Thisbe is one such legend. The claim that it was the blood of the dying Pyramus splashing the mulberry tree which caused it to have a dark colour ever afterwards probably suggested Oberon's story that a hit from Cupid's arrow caused the dark colour of the pansy (II.1.155–68). Several other details in *A Midsummer Night's Dream* come from the *Metamorphoses*, including Titania's name and much of her speech about the disorder of the seasons in Act II Scene 1. Arthur Golding's rather awkward translation of the *Metamorphoses*, made in 1567, including such lines as, 'This said, she took the sword yet warm with slaughter of her love / And setting it beneath her breast, did to her heart it shove' almost certainly suggested the inept verse of 'Pyramus and Thisbe'.

Shakespeare found the Theseus and Hippolyta **plot** in Chaucer's *Knight's Tale*. Here Theseus is styled the 'Duke' of Athens. The poem tells us that he has conquered, captured and wedded the Queen of the Amazons, called 'Ipolita' rather than the usual Antiope, and that he celebrates the occasion with a great feast. The rites of May, the duke's love of hunting with hounds and the names Philostrate and Egeus are all mentioned by Chaucer. Plutarch's *Life of Theseus*, as translated by Sir Thomas North in 1579, seems to have supplied additional details of Theseus's life.

Much of the conception of the fairies must have come from folklore passed on by word of mouth, but some details, particularly those regarding Oberon, derive from a French romance called *Huon of Bordeaux*, which had been translated by Lord Berners between 1533 and 1542, then staged in a dramatised version in 1593, and from a book called *The Discovery of Witchcraft* by Reginald Scot (1584). Apuleius's *Transformations of Lucius* or *The Golden Ass* (a Latin tale of the second-century, translated in 1566 by William Adlington) furnished the ideas of a man turned into an ass who is loved by a superior woman, the punishment of being made to fall in love with an unworthy object, and the recovery of one's true form after a transcendent vision.

There is a wide-ranging account of Shakespeare's literary sources in Harold Brooks's introduction to the Arden edition of *A Midsummer Night's Dream* (1979), which also reprints key extracts in an appendix, and there are helpful evaluations of sources in the New Cambridge edition edited by R.A. Foakes (1984) and in Peter Hollindale's Penguin Critical Study of the play (1992).

Not all of Shakespeare's sources would have existed in the form of books, however. The folklore of the fairies has already been mentioned. The play was undoubtedly influenced also by the courtly pageants staged at country houses. Oberon seems to refer to one of these in the passage where he speaks of seeing 'a mermaid on a dolphin's back' (II.1.150; see Summaries & Commentaries). At Elvetham in 1595, for example, the entertainments laid on for Queen Elizabeth included a water pageant and a group of dancing fairies who gave her a garland of flowers on behalf of 'Auberon the Fairy King'. When Shakespeare's fairies sing and dance, they are probably emulating such well-known occasions and bringing a scaled-down version of the spectacle to the theatre audience.

A more widespread form of festivity which also helped shape the play is the 'rite of May' mentioned by Theseus at IV.1.132, when country folk went out into the woods and hills to celebrate the change of the seasons, particularly young people keen to elude the watchful eye of their elders (see Themes on Marriage). Although 'Maying' was the general name for these customs, they could also be practised at Whitsun and other times of the year, so it is not out of place that Theseus should speak of the rite of May at the end of a midsummer night. Indeed, according to fairy folklore, the summer solstice was a particularly likely time for spirits to appear. Thus the central idea of the liberating night in the wood, when the marital destinies of the lovers are settled, and the fairies' presence is felt, is taken by Shakespeare, not from literary sources, but from popular tradition.

PART SIX

CRITICAL HISTORY &
BROADER PERSPECTIVES

A Midsummer Night's Dream was evidently popular in its author's lifetime. The title page of the first edition (1600) states that it had been 'Sundry times publickely acted', a fact confirmed by Edward Sharpham's comedy *The Fleire*, performed in 1606, which refers familiarly to Thisbe's comical death scene. The text of *A Midsummer Night's Dream* was reprinted in 1619, then in the 1623 First Folio, where a new stage direction at the end of Act III, 'They sleep all the act', has been interpreted by some scholars as indicating a recent revival, since the 'act' seems to have been a musical interlude between scenes which was then newly fashionable.

During the republican period all plays were banned by the government. When the theatres reopened, Shakespeare's works naturally seemed old-fashioned in their language and staging (Samuel Pepys, having seen a 1662 production of the *Dream*, wrote in his diary that it 'was the most insipid ridiculous play that ever I saw in my life'), so to appeal to audiences after the Restoration, *A Midsummer Night's Dream* was put on in rewritten, 'updated' versions, nine of which appeared between 1661 and 1816. In every one, the story was simplified and in the process Shakespeare's careful balance between comedy, love and the supernatural overturned. The creation of character, scene and atmosphere through subtle language was overwhelmed by stunning visual and musical effects. Purcell's opera *The Fairy Queen* (1692), for example, removed half the original text, cutting out Hippolyta and shifting 'Pyramus and Thisbe' to Act III to make way for a big finish, including an appearance by the goddess Juno drawn by peacocks and a grand dance involving monkeys. Garrick's 1755 adaptation, *The Fairies*, cut three quarters of the text, added twenty-seven songs (some imported from other Shakespeare plays) and jettisoned the craftsmen. An 1816 version at Covent Garden added songs, removed Helena from Act I and cut back the lovers' speeches. Again, 'Pyramus and Thisbe' was brought forward to permit a big finish, in this case a pageant of Theseus's triumphs, with the

Minotaur and the ship Argo included in the parade. Traditionally, academics have condemned all this as cultural vandalism, but anyone who has enjoyed such imaginative adaptations of Shakespeare as the 1996 Baz Luhrmann film version of *Romeo and Juliet*, and for that matter the 1999 Michael Hoffman version of *A Midsummer Night's Dream*, will recognise them as ways to make the play fit the production expectations of their day, and to be accessible and entertaining for a contemporary audience who in past centuries would not, after all, have studied Shakespeare in school.

An 1840 production can claim the credit for reinstating about eighty per cent of the original text. Thereafter, actors usually spoke Shakespeare's words, even if some of them were cut, but spectacular costumes, special effects and large amounts of music still predominated – in the second half of the nineteenth century the music normally being Mendelssohn's.

Harley Granville Barker's 1914 version was the first to successfully break with the post-Restoration norm, trying to shift the emphasis from the traditional spectacle to the words themselves. Barker replaced Mendelssohn with English folk music, elaborate sets with painted backdrops and cute fairy costumes with strange gold-painted ones which (in the words of Desmond MacCarthy) made their wearers look 'as if they had been detached from some fantastic, bristling old clock'. There have since been many attempts to present the play afresh while keeping to the original text, among the more radical an American production of 1958 which relocated the play in Texas with the Athenians as cowboys and Hippolyta as a Native American. The best-known such production, because of its systematic attempt to depart from previous stage practices, was Peter Brooks's 1970 version, which made the stage a white box furnished with trapezes and coiled wires, and introduced distinctly adult and libidinous fairies. Hailed by some as an imaginative celebration of theatricality, dismissed by others as mere gimmickry, Brooks's staging certainly made the audience see the play in a new light, but in its way maintained the tradition of striking spectacle. Theatregoers wishing to see the fullest emphasis placed on the power of Shakespeare's text may actually find they are better served by small-scale amateur or semi-professional productions than by those designed to leave their mark on theatrical history.

Much literary criticism of *A Midsummer Night's Dream* has consisted of reactions to its stage history. Critics in the eighteenth and nineteenth century saw the play only in productions which they considered to be heavy-handedly vulgar. Their general view of the play as a piece of writing was that it was a delicate piece of escapism, enjoyable but unstageable, and not to be taken very seriously. Little detailed discussion of it was attempted until the twentieth century, when scholars set about trying to recover something of its original context and to reconstruct its character before it became an excuse for music and dance spectacle.

Studies of folklore such as Minor White Latham's *The Elizabethan Fairies* (Columbia University Press, 1930) and Katherine Briggs's *The Anatomy of Puck* (Routledge & Kegan Paul, 1959) clarified the superstitions on which Shakespeare drew. C.L. Barber in *Shakespeare's Festive Comedy* (Princeton University Press, 1959) related the play to May games, aristocratic pageants and the vogue for Ovid. Paul A. Olson in 'The Meaning of Court Marriage' (1957, see Price 1983), William Rossky in 'Imagination in the English Renaissance' (1958, see Price 1983) and R.W. Dent in 'Imagination in *A Midsummer Night's Dream*' (1964, see Price 1983) interpreted the play in the light of Elizabethan views about the function of imagination.

G. Wilson Knight's *The Shakespearean Tempest* (Methuen, 1932), H.B. Charlton's *Shakespearean Comedy* (Methuen, 1939) and John Russell Brown's *Shakespeare and his Comedies* (Methuen, 1957) integrated the *Dream* into the Shakespeare canon by tracing patterns of imagery, plot device and theme which link it to his other plays. Volumes wholly devoted to the play – David P. Young's *Something of Great Constancy* (Yale University Press, 1966) and Stephen Fender's *Shakespeare: A Midsummer Night's Dream* (Edward Arnold, 1968) – stressed its complexities, showing that it is not simply a pantomime-style entertainment or a repository of Elizabethan beliefs, but a rich text in which the imagination unifies seeming opposites and in which transformation and parody challenge stock responses.

Jan Kott's *Shakespeare Our Contemporary* (Methuen, 1964) offered the most extreme reaction to the traditional view of the play as charming and insubstantial, claiming instead that it depicts a crazed and cruel world, driven by lust. Although refuted by many, Kott's views have certainly been influential (for example, on Peter Brooks's 1970 production) and initiated the late-twentieth-century vogue for 're-readings' of the play in the light of modern preoccupations.

The volume on *A Midsummer Night's Dream* in the Macmillan 'Casebook' series, edited by Antony W. Price (1983) anthologises many of the critics cited above, plus a large number of others. Another highly useful collection is the volume edited by Harold Bloom in the Chelsea House 'Modern Critical Interpretations' series (1987).

RECENT READINGS

Critical approaches in recent decades have tended to focus on those attitudes within the play, such as those toward gender and power, which are most liable to make a modern reader uneasy. One such approach is Feminism, which can range from pointing out male prejudice in a text to arguing that women's experiences produce different values and ways of writing than men's. Shirley Nelson Garner in 'Jack shall have Jill; / Nought shall go ill' (1981, see Dutton 1996) offers a detailed interpretation of the play as a male–female power struggle, while Louis Adrian Montrose's 'Shaping Fantasies: Figurations of Gender and Power in Elizabethan Culture' (1983, see Dutton 1996) relates the presentation of women in *A Midsummer Night's Dream* to Elizabethan men's anxieties about female power, particularly as embodied in their Queen.

Critical approaches to the play do not always fall neatly into separate categories. While Montrose's subject matter is Feminist, his method is actually New Historicist. New Historicists compare works of literature to non-literary writings of the same period in an attempt to understand their original contexts. This approach often overlaps with Marxist studies, which examine how literature has been shaped by the class structures and social changes of its period. Elliot Krieger's *A Marxist Study of Shakespeare's Comedies* (Macmillan, 1979) examines how the apparent contrasts between Theseus's court, on the one hand, and the worlds of the fairies and craftsmen, on the other, actually serve to reinforce the former's assumptions and power. Richard Wilson in 'The Kindly Ones: The Death of the Author in Shakespearean Athens' (1993, see Dutton 1996) sees the play as one in which Shakespeare systematically suppresses any aspect of the story which might challenge the outlook of the ruling class.

A further approach which can be related to Marxism and New Historicism is Dialogics. This considers how a text can come to voice a range of points of view, each questioning the others, rather than be restricted to the limited standpoint of its author. It is sometimes argued that the tradition of multiple points of view, or 'polyphony', arises from festivities such as carnival. In *Shakespeare and the Popular Voice* (Basil Blackwell, 1989), Annabel Patterson suggests that Maying, marriage and the staging of a play are all festive occasions conducive to polyphony, allowing the voices and attitudes of Bottom and the other craftsmen to emerge, despite the fun that is made of them by other characters.

Myth Criticism holds that all literature is ultimately based on myths explaining patterns in nature. Northrop Frye applies this approach to *A Midsummer Night's Dream* in a chapter of *Northrop Frye on Shakespeare* (Yale University Press, 1986), using it to clarify the structure of the comic **plot**, which he also relates to the custom of Maying and to classical mythology.

At the opposite pole to Myth Criticism is Psychoanalytic or Freudian Criticism, which traces the psychological mechanisms by which meaning is created and distorted. Norman Holland in his 'Hermia's Dream' (1979, see Dutton 1996) examines one speech in *A Midsummer Night's Dream* to see what it tells us about the character, how it fits into wider patterns in the text and how the interpretations necessarily reflect the critic's own anxieties. James L. Calderwood in his full-length study of the play in the Twayne/Harvester 'New Critical Introductions to Shakespeare' series (1992) ingeniously brings psychoanalytical and philosophical approaches to bear on a wide range of features. Terence Hawkes in his book *Meaning by Shakespeare* (Routledge, 1993) proposes interpretations of the text which challenge a number of received views. In their concern to open up the text to new readings, both of these critics could loosely be labelled as practitioners of Post-Structuralism, a broad school which starts from the tenet that meaning is not simply inherent in words, but depends on their relation to larger systems of language and thought.

The idea that a text has no single ideal meaning but can validly be interpreted in many ways has proved a challenging one for literary critics, but is an everyday assumption in the theatre and therefore in Theatre Studies. In recent years much valuable work has been done in examining the play in performance, recognising that it is not primarily a text to be read or discussed, but a script requiring theatrical realisation. Roger Warren's *A Midsummer Night's Dream* in the Macmillan 'Text and Performances' series (1983) and Jay L. Halio's equivalent volume in the Manchester University Press 'Shakespeare in Performance' series (1995) give stimulating accounts of performances on stage, television and film. Philip C. McGuire in the opening chapter of his book *Speechless Dialect: Shakespeare's Open Silences* (University of California Press, 1985) examines how different stage productions have dealt with Hippolyta's silences, and so brings us full circle to Feminist concerns.

Garner, Montrose, Krieger, Wilson, Patterson, Holland, Hawkes and McGuire are all anthologised in the Macmillan 'New Casebook' volume edited by Richard Dutton (1996). Linda Cookson and Bryan Loughey have edited a book of original essays on the play for the 'Longman Critical Essays' series (1991) which, written with the needs of students in mind, is inevitably less groundbreaking and more uneven in quality. Helen Hackett's study, *A Midsummer Night's Dream*, in the Northcote House/British Council series 'Writers and their Work' (1997) is an impressive attempt to combine several recent approaches into a brief, accessible study, offering a late-twentieth-century consensus on how the play might be read. Peter Hollindale's volume in the 'Penguin Critical Studies' series (1995) is more traditional in its approach, but is also a perceptive and wide-ranging account.

World events	Shakespeare's life	Literary events
		1385(?) Geoffrey Chaucer, *The Knight's Tale*
1455 First printed book in Europe		
		1516 Thomas More, *Utopia*
		1532 Machiavelli, *The Prince*
		1533-42 *Huon of Bordeaux*, translated by Lord Berners
1534 Church of England breaks with Rome		
	1557 John Shakespeare marries Mary Arden	
1558 Elizabeth I becomes Queen		
	1564 William Shakespeare is born	
		1566 William Adlington's translation of Apuleius's *Golden Ass*
		1567 Golding's translation of Ovid's *Metamorphoses*
1576 First theatre in England opens at Shoreditch		
		1579 Sir Thomas North's translation of Plutarch's *Life of Theseus*
1582 Plague breaks out in London	**1582** Shakespeare marries Anne Hathaway	
1583 Newfoundland is claimed for Elizabeth I by Gilbert	**1583** A daughter, Susanna, is born	
		1584 Reginald Scott, *The Discovery of Witchcraft*
	1585 The twins, Hamnet and Judith, are born	
	late **1580s** - early **1590s** Shakespeare probably writes *Henry VI*, parts I, II & III and *Richard III*	
1588 Spanish Armada defeated		
	1592 Shakespeare acting in London	
	1592-4 He writes *The Comedy of Errors*	
	1594 *Love's Labour's Lost* written; Shakespeare writes exclusively for the Lord Chamberlain's Men	
1595-1603 Tyrone's rebellion in Ireland	**1595** *Two Gentlemen of Verona, The Taming of the Shrew* and *Love's Labours Lost* are thought to have been completed by this time. He writes *A Midsummer Nights Dream*	

World events	Shakespeare's life	Literary events
1596 Francis Drake perishes on an expedition to the West Indies	**1596-8** *Henry IV*, parts 1 & 2 written	
1598 First mention of the game of cricket	**1598** *As You Like It*	
	1598-9 Globe Theatre built at Southwark	
	1599 *Henry V* completed	
	1600 *A Midsummer Night's Dream, Much Ado about Nothing* and *The Merchant of Venice* printed. *Twelfth Night* and *Julius Caesar* probably written	
	1600-1 *Hamlet* written	
	1602 *Troilus and Cressida* probably written	
1603 Elizabeth I dies	**1603** His company becomes the King's Men, patronised by James I, the new king	
	1604 *Othello* performed	**1604** James I, *A Counterblast to Tobacco*
1605 Discovery of Guy Fawkes' plot to destroy Parliament	**1605** First version of *King Lear*	**1605** Cervantes, *Don Quixote*
	1606 Shakespeare writes *Macbeth*	**1606** Ben Johnson, *Volpone;* Edward Sharpham, *The Fleire*
	1606-7 *Antony and Cleopatra* probably written	
	1608 The King's Men acquire Blackfriar's Theatre for winter performances	
1610 Use of the fork for eating spreads from Italy to England	**1610** *Coriolanus* written	
	1611 *The Tempest* written; Shakespeare retires to his house in Stratford	
1612 Last burning of heretics in England		**1612** John Webster, *The White Devil*
	1613 Globe Theatre burns down	
	1616 Shakespeare dies	
1620 The Mayflower takes the Pilgrim Fathers to Massachusetts		
	1623 First collected volume of Shakespeare's plays published	
		1692 Henry Purcell, *The Fairy Queen*

alliteration a sequence of repeated consonantal sounds, usually at the beginnings of words or stressed syllables. The sound pattern may reinforce patterns of meaning in the language. 'Following *d*arkness like a *d*ream' (V.1.376)

antithesis the placing of contrasting ideas in adjacent clauses or sentences, using parallel forms of words. 'Since night you loved me; yet since night you left me' (III.2.275)

ballad a song or poem which tells a story in simple, colloquial language, using a traditional verse form. In Shakespeare's *The Winter's Tale* (IV.4), Autolycus sells eager countryfolk ballads recounting stories which he claims are true and which are certainly no less fantastic than Bottom's transformation and encounter with the Fairy Queen

blank verse unrhymed iambic pentameter; the normal metre of Elizabethan drama. Its popularity is due to its flexibility and relative closeness to the rhythms of spoken English

characterisation the way in which a writer creates characters so as to convey their personalities effectively, attract or repel our sympathies and integrate their behaviour into the story

comedy a broad genre; the word is most often used to describe a drama which is intended primarily to entertain the audience and which ends happily for the main characters. In this meaning of the word, 'comedy', like tragedy, is an ancient dramatic form dating at least as far back as the fifth century BC. It probably originated in the seasonal festivities, often obscene, which were part of the Dionysiac fertility cult. The most notable writers of comedy among the ancient Greeks were Aristophanes, whose plays combine lyrical poetry, buffoonery, satire and fantastical plots and characters, and Menander, who is only known because of his strong influence on the Roman playwrights Plautus and Terence. Their comedies are more social in their focus, contain songs, and have elaborate plots involving stock characters, such as spendthrift young men and wily servants, many of whom were copied by Renaissance playwrights. Shakespeare's *The Comedy of Errors*, for example, is modelled on the *Menaechmi* of Plautus.

Most comedies from the Renaissance until the present day share certain features: they do not concentrate on the fortunes of an individual, but the interest is spread over a group of people; they tend to deal with low life and humble people, rather than with kings and nobles; their plots are usually elaborate, involve misunderstandings and deceptions, and move from the possibility of disaster towards a happy ending, often symbolised by a wedding

counterpoint combining two or more musical parts so that they are heard simultaneously. By extension, combining different things (such as the stories which make up *A Midsummer Night's Dream*) so that comparison, contrast and interaction between them create an overall effect which is more powerful than any of them would produce independently

couplet a pair of rhymed lines

end-stopped line a line of verse in which the end of the line coincides with an essential grammatical pause

genre the term for a kind or type of literature, such as ballad, comedy or tragedy

iambic pentameter an iamb is the commonest metrical foot in English verse, consisting of a weakly stressed syllable, followed by a strongly stressed syllable. An iambic pentameter is a line of five iambic feet: 'Four *days* / will *quick* / ly *steep* / them*selves* / in *night*' (I.1.7). Occasionally a trochee (a strongly stressed syllable, followed by a weakly stressed one) may be substituted for one of the iambs, particularly at the beginning of a line, either for emphasis or to prevent monotony: '*Happy* / be *The* / seus, *our* / re*nown* / ed *Duke*' (I.1.20)

imagery, image in its narrowest sense, an 'image' is a word-picture, describing some visible scene or object, like Oberon's description beginning, 'I know a bank where the wild thyme blows' (II.1.249). More commonly, 'imagery' refers to the figurative language (metaphors and similes) in a piece of literature – 'The iron tongue of midnight hath told twelve' (V.1.353) – or even all the words which appeal to the senses: 'And neigh, and bark, and grunt and roar and burn' (III.1.104)

lyric in Greek verse, a lyric is a song to be accompanied by the lyre. Hence the words of a song are still called 'lyrics'. More generally, the term is applied to poetry which is neither narrative nor dramatic, but which expresses the feelings and thoughts of an individual speaker, particularly in relation to the subject of love

metaphor a metaphor goes further than a comparison between two different things or ideas by fusing them together: one thing is described as being another thing, carrying over its associations: 'to see the sails conceive / And grow big-bellied with the wanton wind' (II.1.128–9)

metre the use of a linguistic feature which, repeated, creates a sense of pattern, distinguishing verse from prose. In English verse the commonest such pattern is stress- or accent-based metre, which consists of a regular arrangement of strong stresses in a stretch of language (see iambic pentameter)

pastoral a genre which originated in Greece in the third century BC, describing an imaginary world of simple, idealised rural life, in which shepherds and shepherdesses fall in love, enjoying a life of blissful ease, singing songs, playing the flute, and so on. The pastoral usually deals with a perfect world, set far back in time and inhabited by gods, goddesses and other supernatural beings such as nymphs. Shakespeare uses some of the conventions of pastoral in his comedy *As You Like It*, written a few years after *A Midsummer Night's Dream*

personification a variety of figurative or metaphorical language in which things or ideas are treated as if they were human beings, with human attributes and feelings: 'Phoebe doth behold / Her silver visage in the watery glass' (I.1.209)

plot the plan of a literary work. More than the simple sequence of events, 'plot' suggests a pattern of relationships between events: a story with a beginning, middle and end, with its various parts bound together by cause and effect, exhibiting a version of typical experience or a view of morality. Suspense is vital to make a plot entertaining: we should be made to want to know what is going to happen, and be surprised by new incidents, yet be satisfied that they grow logically out of what we already know. More loosely, 'plot' may refer to the separate narratives within one larger story. For example, Elizabethan drama commonly features a 'main plot' and a 'subplot'. Unusually, *A Midsummer Night's Dream* contains three plots of roughly equal importance: the lovers' tribulations, the quarrel between the Fairy King and Queen, and the struggle to stage 'Pyramus and Thisbe'

prose any language which is not made patterned by some kind of metre

quatrain a stanza of four lines

register a variety of language which is used in a particular situation: for example, the language of law or of newspaper headlines

rhetoric rhetoric is the art of writing and speaking effectively so as to persuade an audience. Ancient and medieval scholars classified various devices of language which might be employed to achieve particular rhetorical effects. Among these 'rhetorical figures' still commonly cited are, for example, alliteration and antithesis

satire literature which exhibits or examines vice and folly and directs laughter against them to make them appear ridiculous or contemptible

simile an explicit comparison in which one thing is said to be like another. Similes always contain the words 'like' or 'as': 'Swift as a shadow, short as any dream' (I.1.144)

soliloquy the convention in which a character in a play speaks directly to the audience, as if thinking aloud about their motives, feelings and decisions

sonnet a lyric poem, consisting of fourteen lines of iambic pentameter, rhymed and organised according to one of several intricate schemes. A book of 154 sonnets by Shakespeare was published in 1609, probably without his permission

stock character or figure a type of character who recurs in a genre, and may even be one of its defining features. A father determined to prevent his daughter's marriage and lovers who attempt to elope are figures found in many stories, including *A Midsummer Night's Dream* and *Romeo and Juliet*

symbol something which represents something else (often an idea or quality) either by analogy or association. Many symbols exist by convention and tradition. According to different conventions, a serpent may stand for wisdom or for evil. The latter is the case in *A Midsummer Night's Dream* II.1.9, II.2.152–5 and V.1.423. Writers also develop their own symbols, sometimes using them as a species of metaphor in which the exact subject of the metaphor is not made explicit and may be open to a variety of readings: for example, the moon in this play (see Imagery & Symbolism)

theme the abstract subject of a work; its central idea or ideas, which may or may not be explicit or obvious. A text may contain several themes or thematic interests

tragedy, tragic a story, usually a play, which traces the downfall of an individual, and shows in so doing both the capacities and limitations of human life

trochaic tetrameter a trochee is a metrical foot, consisting of a strongly stressed syllable, followed by a weakly stressed syllable. A trochaic tetrameter is a line of four trochaic feet, sometimes (as here) with the final syllable omitted: '*Now* the / *hun*gry / *li*on / *roars*' (V.1.361)

verse poetry, especially metrical writing

wit originally meaning 'sense', 'understanding' or 'intelligence' ('if I had wit enough to get out of this wood', III.1.141–2), during the seventeenth century the word came to refer specifically to that kind of poetic intelligence which combines or contrasts ideas and expressions in an unexpected and intellectually pleasing manner

AUTHOR OF THIS NOTE

Michael Sherborne is Curriculum Manager of English at Luton Sixth Form College. He is the author of the York Notes Advanced on *Brave New World* (2000) and *Nineteen Eighty-Four* (2001). He has edited *The Country of the Blind and Other Stories by H. G. Wells* (Oxford University Press, not available in the EC, 1996) and is the author of *Modern Novelists: H. G. Wells* (Macmillan/St. Martin's Press, 1987), written under his previous name, Michael Draper.

GCSE and equivalent levels

Maya Angelou
I Know Why the Caged Bird Sings

Jane Austen
Pride and Prejudice

Alan Ayckbourn
Absent Friends

Elizabeth Barrett Browning
Selected Poems

Robert Bolt
A Man for All Seasons

Harold Brighouse
Hobson's Choice

Charlotte Brontë
Jane Eyre

Emily Brontë
Wuthering Heights

Shelagh Delaney
A Taste of Honey

Charles Dickens
David Copperfield

Charles Dickens
Great Expectations

Charles Dickens
Hard Times

Charles Dickens
Oliver Twist

Roddy Doyle
Paddy Clarke Ha Ha Ha

George Eliot
Silas Marner

George Eliot
The Mill on the Floss

William Golding
Lord of the Flies

Oliver Goldsmith
She Stoops To Conquer

Willis Hall
The Long and the Short and the Tall

Thomas Hardy
Far from the Madding Crowd

Thomas Hardy
The Mayor of Casterbridge

Thomas Hardy
Tess of the d'Urbervilles

Thomas Hardy
The Withered Arm and other Wessex Tales

L.P. Hartley
The Go-Between

Seamus Heaney
Selected Poems

Susan Hill
I'm the King of the Castle

Barry Hines
A Kestrel for a Knave

Louise Lawrence
Children of the Dust

Harper Lee
To Kill a Mockingbird

Laurie Lee
Cider with Rosie

Arthur Miller
The Crucible

Arthur Miller
A View from the Bridge

Robert O'Brien
Z for Zachariah

Frank O'Connor
My Oedipus Complex and other stories

George Orwell
Animal Farm

J.B. Priestley
An Inspector Calls

Willy Russell
Educating Rita

Willy Russell
Our Day Out

J.D. Salinger
The Catcher in the Rye

William Shakespeare
Henry IV Part 1

William Shakespeare
Henry V

William Shakespeare
Julius Caesar

William Shakespeare
Macbeth

William Shakespeare
The Merchant of Venice

William Shakespeare
A Midsummer Night's Dream

William Shakespeare
Much Ado About Nothing

William Shakespeare
Romeo and Juliet

William Shakespeare
The Tempest

William Shakespeare
Twelfth Night

George Bernard Shaw
Pygmalion

Mary Shelley
Frankenstein

R.C. Sherriff
Journey's End

Rukshana Smith
Salt on the snow

John Steinbeck
Of Mice and Men

Robert Louis Stevenson
Dr Jekyll and Mr Hyde

Jonathan Swift
Gulliver's Travels

Robert Swindells
Daz 4 Zoe

Mildred D. Taylor
Roll of Thunder, Hear My Cry

Mark Twain
Huckleberry Finn

James Watson
Talking in Whispers

William Wordsworth
Selected Poems

A Choice of Poets

Mystery Stories of the Nineteenth Century including The Signalman

Nineteenth Century Short Stories

Poetry of the First World War

Six Women Poets

York Notes Advanced

Margaret Atwood
Cat's Eye

Margaret Atwood
The Handmaid's Tale

Jane Austen
Mansfield Park

Jane Austen
Persuasion

Jane Austen
Pride and Prejudice

Alan Bennett
Talking Heads

William Blake
Songs of Innocence and of Experience

Charlotte Brontë
Jane Eyre

Emily Brontë
Wuthering Heights

Angela Carter
Nights at the Circus

Geoffrey Chaucer
The Franklin's Tale

Geoffrey Chaucer
The Miller's Prologue and Tales

Geoffrey Chaucer
Prologue To the Canterbury Tales

Geoffrey Chaucer
The Wife of Bath's Prologue and Tale

Joseph Conrad
Heart of Darkness

Charles Dickens
Great Expectations

Charles Dickens
Hard Times

Emily Dickinson
Selected Poems

John Donne
Selected Poems

Carol Ann Duffy
Selected Poems

George Eliot
Middlemarch

George Eliot
The Mill on the Floss

T.S. Eliot
Selected Poems

F. Scott Fitzgerald
The Great Gatsby

E.M. Forster
A Passage to India

Brian Friel
Translations

Thomas Hardy
The Mayor of Casterbridge

Thomas Hardy
The Return of the Native

Thomas Hardy
Selected Poems

Thomas Hardy
Tess of the d'Urbervilles

Seamus Heaney
Selected Poems from Opened Ground

Nathaniel Hawthorne
The Scarlet Letter

Kazou Ishiguro
The Remains of the Day

James Joyce
Dubliners

John Keats
Selected Poems

Christopher Marlowe
Doctor Faustus

Arthur Miller
Death of a Salesman

John Milton
Paradise Lost Books I & II

Toni Morrison
Beloved

William Shakespeare
Antony and Cleopatra

William Shakespeare
As You Like It

William Shakespeare
Hamlet

William Shakespeare
King Lear

William Shakespeare
Measure for Measure

William Shakespeare
The Merchant of Venice

William Shakespeare
A Midsummer Night's Dream

William Shakespeare
Much Ado About Nothing

William Shakespeare
Othello

William Shakespeare
Richard II

William Shakespeare
Romeo and Juliet

William Shakespeare
The Taming of the Shrew

William Shakespeare
The Tempest

William Shakespeare
The Winter's Tale

George Bernard Shaw
Saint Joan

Mary Shelley
Frankenstein

Alice Walker
The Color Purple

Oscar Wilde
The Importance of Being Earnest

Tennessee Williams
A Streetcar Named Desire

John Webster
The Duchess of Malfi

Virginia Woolf
To the Lighthouse

W.B. Yeats
Selected Poems

.